Common Core
ENGLISH GRAMMAR 6
& Mechanics

Nancy L. McGraw
Nancy Tondy
Regina Webb

Joan Archer
Diane Dillon
Patricia Kecskemety

Bright Ideas Press, LLC
Cleveland, OH

Summer Solutions
Common Core
English Grammar & Mechanics 6

All rights reserved. No part of this publication may be reproduced or transmitted in any form or by any means, electronic or mechanical, including photocopy, recording, or any information storage or retrieval system. Reproduction of these materials for an entire class, school, or district is prohibited.

Printed in the United States of America

The writers of *Summer Solutions* Common Core English Grammar & Mechanics aligned the series in accordance with information from the following:

National Governors Association Center for Best Practices,
Council of Chief State School Officers.
Common Core State Standards, English Language Arts.
National Governors Association Center for Best Practices,
Council of Chief State School Officers, Washington, D.C., 2010.

ISBN: 978-1-60873-063-6

Cover Design: Dan Mazzola
Editor: Christopher Backs

Copyright © 2015 by Bright Ideas Press, LLC
Cleveland, Ohio

Instructions for Parents / Guardians

- *Summer Solutions* is an extension of the *Simple Solutions* Approach being used by thousands of children in schools across the United States.

- This summer book aligns with the English Language Arts Common Core State Standards, which identify key ideas, understandings, and skills appropriate for this particular grade level. The Common Core State Standards addressed in this book are listed on the next page.

- The 30 lessons included in each workbook are meant to review and reinforce the skills learned in the grade level just completed.

- The program is designed to be used three days per week for ten weeks to ensure retention. Completing the book all at one time defeats the purpose of sustained practice over the summer break.

- The answers for each lesson are found in the back of the book. Lessons should be checked immediately after completion for optimal feedback. Items that were difficult for students or done incorrectly should be resolved right away to ensure mastery.

- Help Pages (also toward the back of the book) list the parts of speech, punctuation and capitalization rules, and other information meant to help students complete the lessons independently.

- Adjust the use of the book to fit vacations. More lessons may have to be completed during the weeks before or following a family vacation.

Summer Solutions
Common Core
English Grammar & Mechanics 6

Reviewed Skills Include	Standard
• Ensure that pronouns are in the proper case	L.6.1a
• Use intensive pronouns	L.6.1b
• Recognize and correct inappropriate shifts in pronoun number and person	L.6.1c
• Recognize and correct vague pronouns	L.6.1d
• Use punctuation to set off nonrestrictive/parenthetical elements	L.6.2a
• Spell grade-appropriate words	L.6.2b
• Vary sentence patterns for meaning, reader/listener interest, and style	L.6.3a
• Maintain consistency in style and tone	L.6.3b
• Use context as a clue to the meaning of a word or phrase	L.6.4a
• Use common, grade-appropriate Greek and Latin affixes and roots	L.6.4b
• Consult reference materials	L.6.4c
• Interpret figures of speech	L.6.5a
• Use the relationship between particular words to better understand each of the words	L.6.5b
• Distinguish among the connotations of words with similar denotations	L.6.5c

Help Pages begin on page 63.

Answers to Lessons begin on page 77.

Lesson #1

1. **The simple subject has no modifiers. The complete subject includes the simple subject plus all of the modifiers that go with it.** Underline the simple subject in each sentence.

    A little red <u>lighthouse</u> is the subject of a picture book by Hildegarde Swift. <u>Fans</u> of the book saved the lighthouse. Happily, it is still standing today.

2. Read the sentence below. Choose the meaning of the underlined word.

    The angry lifeguard blew her whistle and shouted using a <u>strident</u> tone.

    hushed   (polite)   harsh

3. **A subject pronoun is used as the subject of a sentence. Object pronouns replace nouns in the predicate of a sentence.** Complete each sentence with a pronoun. Write S if it is a *subject pronoun* or O if it is an *object pronoun*.

    We looked at the new uniforms. The colors surprised _____.   O

    The girls need a ride home. Can you drive _____?   O

    _____ walk their dog every day after school.   S

4. Draw a line through the sentence fragment.

    Summer vacation had just started. I couldn't wait to sleep in, ride my bike, and swim. ~~The fun things of summer.~~

5. Add some words to make the fragment in item 4 into a sentence.

    There are so many fun things of summer.

6. **The verb is the main word in the predicate.** Underline the verb.

   The batter usually <u>takes</u> a few warm up swings.

7. **Coordinating conjunctions join words, clauses, or phrases that are equal in a sentence.** Complete the sentence with a coordinating conjunction.

   A red pick-up truck __and__ a silver camper collided on the interstate.

8. The nouns have been underlined in each sentence. Write C above each *common* noun and P above each *proper* noun.

   <u>Lena</u>(P) went to a <u>bakery</u>(C) in <u>Paris</u>(P) to buy a <u>macaron</u>(C) for <u>dessert</u>(C).

   <u>Paul</u>(P) took the <u>basket</u>(C) out of his <u>Kia</u>(P) and set it on the <u>ground</u>(C).

9. Choose the correct spelling of each word to complete the sentence.

   The red scarf is a fine (compliment / **complement**) to your pink blouse.
   Thanks, I received many (**compliments** / complements) on this outfit.

10. **A preposition relates a noun or pronoun to the rest of the sentence.**

    Example: Sofia is buying a present <u>at</u> the mall.

    Underline the preposition and circle the object of the preposition.

    Champ buries bones <u>under</u> his (doghouse).

Lesson #2

1. **A possessive pronoun shows ownership. It takes the place of a possessive noun.** Use a possessive pronoun to complete each sentence.

   Every time Ella petted our neighbor's dog, it wagged ____its____ tail.

   The birds flapped ____their____ wings as they soared overhead.

   Dad asked, "Do you remember where I parked ____the____ car?

2. **A subordinating conjunction joins a subordinate clause to a main clause.**

   Example: Mick will drive us <u>unless he has to meet his brother</u>.

   Underline the subordinate clause. Double underline the subordinating conjunction.

   <u>Since it is the birthplace of Abraham Lincoln</u>, Springfield holds a Presidents' Day parade every year.

3. Choose the correct spelling of each word to complete the sentence.

   (**You're**/ Your) invited to a rodeo. It sounds like fun, and you can wear (you're / **your**) cowboy hat.

4. Complete the compound predicate with a coordinating conjunction.

   The food truck is still selling fresh doughnuts ____but____ is out of muffins.

5. Read the sentence below. Choose the meaning of the underlined word.

   Marcia was happy and <u>ebullient</u> about riding her new bike to school.

   disinterested   **enthusiastic**   grumpy

6. Underline each subject pronoun and circle each object pronoun in the sentences.

   Nora wrote a poem for (me). <u>She</u> was only twelve years old when *Teen Magazine* published (it).

   <u>They</u> asked Henry to clean the garage for (them). "I can clean the garage if Candace will give Fido's dinner to (him)," Henry replied.

7. Circle the preposition.

   The bus is driving the <u>soccer team</u> (to) the state <u>tournament</u>.

   The object of the preposition is ___to___.

8. Match each underlined word to the reason it is capitalized.

   __C__ <u>Let's</u> go to the movies.   A) proper adjective

   __D__ Lori and <u>I</u> share a locker.   B) brand name

   __B__ I bought you a <u>Snickers</u>.   C) first word of a sentence

   __A__ The <u>Saturday</u> hikes are fun.   D) personal pronoun I

9. **Adjectives describe nouns or pronouns.** Underline the adjectives in the sentence below.

   An <u>old</u>, <u>slow</u> tractor plowed up the <u>dry</u>, <u>brittle</u> stalks last Sunday.

10. **The simple predicate is the verb; the complete predicate is the verb plus all the words that modify it.** Underline the simple predicate in each sentence.

    The people of France <u>gave</u> the Statue of Liberty to the United States. Today the statue <u>celebrates</u> liberty and the friendship between the U.S. and France.

Lesson #3

1. **If a word or phrase is nonrestrictive, it can be removed without changing the meaning of the sentence.** Place a comma before and after a nonrestrictive word or phrase.

   Garrett is so excited about the trip, a Greek island cruise, that he has already begun to pack.

2. Choose the correct spelling of each word to complete the sentences.

   They enjoyed a bowl of their favorite (**cereal** / serial) for breakfast.
   A chapter of the (cereal / **serial**) novel appeared each week in the paper.

   The knight was about to (sleigh / **slay**) the dragon.
   Santa's elves loaded his (**sleigh** / slay) with treats for the reindeer.

3. **A reflexive pronoun renames an antecedent within a sentence. It cannot be removed without changing the meaning of the sentence.** Underline each reflexive pronoun and draw an arrow to its antecedent.

   Example: She even impressed <u>herself</u> with all her blue ribbons.

   Green plants produce <u>food</u> for themselves.

   Cell division is the process in which a cell makes a copy of itself.

4. **An intensive pronoun emphasizes the antecedent; it can be removed without changing the meaning of the sentence.**

   Underline the intensive pronoun and circle its antecedent.

   (Wyatt) scored all the ice hockey goals <u>himself</u>.

5. Underline the simple subject and circle the simple predicate.

   The (line) for the twistiest roller coaster <u>wound</u> around the park.

6. Draw a line through the fragment and rewrite it as a complete sentence on the line. What is missing from the fragment?

   (subject)   verb

   Rodney and Tom went fishing on the Cuyahoga River. Caught a catfish, a few carp, and a trout. They threw all the fish back in the river.

   Rodney caught a catfish, a few carp, and a trout

7. Form the present progressive tense using the verb *start*.

   Amelia's little sister ____is starting____ kindergarten in the fall.

8. **A prepositional phrase begins with a preposition and ends with a noun or pronoun.**
   Example: Crystal went to the meeting *instead of me.*
                                           preposition   object of the preposition

   Read the sentence and write the correct words on the lines.

   Isabel opened the book and gently tucked the letter between its pages.

   preposition __between__   object of the preposition __pages__

9. **Correlative conjunctions work in pairs to join words.** Choose a correlative conjunction pair to complete the sentence.

   Neither / nor   As / as   If / then

   ____Neither____ sub zero temperatures ____nor____ driving snow could keep Amanda from skiing every weekend.

10. Identify each type of sentence.

    __B__ Bundle up.   A) exclamatory

    __A__ Stop that thief!   B) imperative

Lesson #4

1. Form the underline{future progressive} tense using the verb *prepare*.

   The chef _____will be preparing_____ cheese ravioli as today's special pasta.

2. Are the underlined words synonyms or antonyms?

   The melodious sounds coming from the music room were suddenly replaced by discordant bickering.

           synonyms   <u>antonyms</u>

3. Match each pronoun example with its type.

   I found his phone yesterday and returned it to him today. He thanked
         A   B   C

   me over and over. He had convinced himself that it was lost forever.
                                         D

   __C__ subject pronoun   __B__ object pronoun

   __D__ reflexive pronoun   __A__ possessive pronoun

4. **A collective noun takes a singular verb.** Underline the collective noun and choose the verb that agrees.

   A <u>pack</u> of wild ponies (roam / **roams**) freely on Assateague Island.

5. **A pronoun must agree with its antecedent in number.**

   Incorrect: The **team** chose green and white for **their** away uniform.
   (The antecedent is singular, but the pronoun is plural.)

   Correct: The **team** chose green and white for **its** away uniform.
   (Both the antecedent and the pronoun are singular.)

   Write the correct pronoun for each sentence. Circle the verb that agrees.

   The bakery is open late, but ____it____ often (run / **runs**) out of bagels.

   The students (**elect** / elects) to hold ____their____ meetings on Mondays.

6. **Personification is a literary device in which an animal or an object is given human features.**

    Example: Every fall, <u>maples paint</u> the forest floor in bright colors.

    Underline the personification in each sentence.

    The <u>page winced</u> as Samantha tore it in half.

    <u>Rain pounded its fists</u> against the window pane.

7. Complete the compound sentence with a coordinating conjunction.

    Seraphina wondered if she should join the river clean-up team, ___or___ if she should volunteer at the senior center.

8. Underline the complete predicate; circle the simple predicate.

    Everyone who does not play an instrument <u>will ⓢⓘⓝⓖ in the choir</u>.

9. **An indefinite pronoun must agree with other pronouns in a sentence. See the *Help Pages* for a list of indefinite pronouns.** Underline the indefinite pronoun and circle the possessive pronoun that agrees with it.

    Our cats don't seem hungry today. I wonder why <u>neither</u>, ate all of (ⓘⓣⓢ / their) kibble.

10. Insert commas after the introductory words.

    Oh no, I left the water on!
    Hurry, I've got to get back home.

Lesson #5

1. Insert commas to separate words or phrases in a series.

   We played beach volleyball, swam in the ocean, and roasted marshmallows on our first day of vacation.

2. Choose the correlative conjunction pair that best completes the sentence.

   whether / or   not only / but also   if / then   neither / nor

   Since I don't have much money this week, I can ____neither____ buy concert tickets ____nor____ go to the opening day ball game.

3. Underline the adjectives in the sentence below.

   An <u>enormous</u> <u>golden</u> dog poked its <u>cold</u>, <u>wet</u> nose through a hole in the <u>rotten</u> <u>wooden</u> fence.

4. Underline the prepositional phrase; write the object of the preposition.

   Avalanche danger increases when skiers ski <u>outside the boundaries</u>.

   ____ski____

5. **A noun can be a direct object in a sentence. The direct object receives the action of the verb.**

   Example: The judge <u>pinned</u> the blue (ribbon) on the dog's collar.
   (Ask: What did the judge pin?   ribbon)

   Underline the verb in each sentence. Circle the direct object.

   Jerome <u>bought</u> a baseball (mitt). Carina <u>baked</u> (tarts) for the bake sale.

6. **Adverbs modify verbs by telling *how*, *when*, *where*, or *to what extent*.** Circle the adverb and underline the verb it modifies.

    The cyclist braked quickly.

    In which way does it modify the verb? _____

7. In each sentence, underline the prepositional phrase; write the object of the preposition.

    A collie had chased the squirrel into our yard. _____

    The squirrel scrambled up the oak tree and disappeared. _____

8. Form the past progressive tense using the verb *rise*.

    The river _____ before the snow began to melt.

9. Use a dictionary to match the correct spelling of each word with its definition.

alter	a table or raised platform used for worship
altar	a verb meaning to change something
mussel	a noun referring to body tissue that produces movement
muscle	a shellfish

10. Rewrite these words with the suffixes.

    study + ous → *studious*   enjoy + able → *enjoyable*

    pay + ment → *payment*   imply + ed → *implied*

Lesson #6

1. Choose the correct homophone to complete each sentence.

   affect: (verb) to influence or act upon

   effect: (noun) end result; produced by a cause

   A) An (affect / effect) of climate change may be warmer oceans.
   B) Warmer oceans will (affect / effect) aquatic animals.

2. Draw a line through the fragment.

   Christopher published his first short story when he was still in middle school. The story, "Two Spinning Wheels," appeared in a cycling magazine. Lots of adventure and intrigue on a bicycle. You should read it.

3. Add some words to make the fragment in the above item into a sentence.

   _____

   _____

4. **A present perfect verb shows action that is ongoing or indefinite.** Complete the sentences by adding the <u>present perfect form</u> of the verb *prepare*.

   Alyssa _____ paella for dinner.

   Her friends _____ a variety of tapas.

5. Choose the correlative conjunction pair that best completes the sentence.

       Whether / or   Not only / but also   If / then   Neither / nor

   _____ we are going to get home before the ice cream melts,

   _____ we better hurry.

6. Make one sentence with a compound predicate.

   Aiden and Levi are in the same gym class. Aiden and Levi play on the same rugby team.

   _____

   _____

7. **A transitive verb shows action and has a direct object.** Underline the transitive verb and draw a star over the direct object.

   Every student brought two sharpened pencils to the test.

8. Find the meaning of the word *discerning* in a dictionary. Put a check next to the statement that is true.

   _____ Discerning is the same as unobservant.
   _____ A person who is discerning shows good judgment.
   _____ Being discerning means creating a disturbance.

   What part of speech is the word *discerning*? _____

9. Cross out an inappropriate shift in verb tense and write the correct word above it.

   The car has two flat tires and was out of gas.

10. **A prepositional phrase may come between the subject and verb.**

    Example: The snow *on the mountain peaks* (melts) sometime in July.

    Underline the simple subject. Choose the verb that agrees.

    The dogs in the kennel (has / (have)) eaten.

Lesson #7

1. Match each word to a part of the *i before e except after c or when sounding like 'a'* spelling rule.

   weight   i before e

   conceive   except after c

   thief   or when sounding like 'a'

2. Choose the correct spelling of each word.

   If we tie the hammock to these trees we can (lie / lay) in the shade.

   Let's (lie / lay) a pillow on this end, so we can both nap.

3. Underline the prepositional phrase and circle the preposition.

   The bicycle rally began behind the elementary school.

   Write the object of the preposition. _____

4. Put a check next to any prefix that means "not."

   ____ im- (impractical)   ____ re- (reapply)

   ____ dis- (discourteous)   ____ non- (nonnegotiable)

   ____ post- (postpone)   ____ in- (inapplicable)

5. **An idiom is a saying with a figurative — not literal — meaning.** Write the letter of the meaning next to each idiom.

   __E__ spill the beans   A) study

   __F__ cost an arm and a leg   B) work harder

   __A__ hit the books   C) from one difficulty to another

   __B__ apply some elbow grease   D) undecided

   __D__ on the fence   E) tell a secret

   __C__ out of the pot, into the fire   F) very expensive

6. Write the <u>future progressive</u> tense of the verb *dance*.

   Gabriella _____ in the holiday ballet.

7. Underline the reflexive pronoun and circle its antecedent.

   Cats are known to groom themselves as well as other cats.

8. The nouns have been underlined in each sentence. Write C above each *common* noun and P above each *proper* noun.

   The <u>kids</u> received <u>baskets</u> with <u>Snickers</u>, <u>Kit Kats</u>, and chocolate <u>rabbits</u> for <u>Easter</u>.

9. **If a phrase is restrictive, you cannot remove it without changing the meaning of the sentence. Commas are not needed around a restrictive phrase.**

   Circle the restrictive phrase. Insert commas around the nonrestrictive phrase.

   Today *by the way* is the day we turn in our library books.

   Practice *on Saturday morning* will start an hour early.

10. **The denotation of a word is its literal meaning.** What is the denotation of the word *clever*?

    _____

Lesson #8

1. **Avoid using a pronoun when the pronoun makes the meaning unclear.**

   Unclear: Ethan took Paul fishing because it was *his* birthday.
   Clear: Ethan took Paul fishing because it was *Paul's* birthday.

   Write an improved version of the sentence below.

   Grace called Alex so she could tell her the homework assignment.

   _____

2. Read the following quote from *The Yearling*.

   "The water made a sound like kittens lapping."
   ~ Marjorie Kinnan Rawlings

   What type of figure of speech is the quote? _____

3. Use a subordinating conjunction to complete each sentence.

   | before | until | except | unless |

   The new driver fastened his seatbelt and adjusted the rearview mirror _____ starting the car.

   Mom will bake peanut butter cookies _____ someone has a peanut allergy.

4. Use the past progressive form of the indicated verb in each sentence.

   The cows _____ in the shade of a weeping willow.
   (lie)

   The baby _____ when all the dogs started barking.
   (sleep)

5. **Use context clues to figure out the meaning of a word. Use a dictionary or thesaurus to find the word's exact meanings.**

   Due to her *congenial* nature, Dawn always had many friends.

   Circle the words that are synonyms of *congenial*.

   aloof   amiable   friendly   affable

6. Correctly spell these plural words.

   halfs _____   boxs _____   tomato _____

7 – 8. **Words can evoke certain feelings or reactions. This is called the word's *connotation*.**

   Antonia is such a <u>chicken</u> that she will not touch the turtle's shell.

   What is the denotation of the underlined word? _____

   What is the connotation in the sentence? _____

9 – 10. Read the sentences. Identify the function of each word.

   A gentle <u>wind</u> <u>blew</u> the sleek new <u>boat</u> out onto the
          A   B   C

   open sea. <u>It</u> <u>was</u> a beautiful day to be <u>on</u> the <u>water</u>.
            D E   F   G

   ____ object of the preposition   ____ preposition

   ____ direct object   ____ linking verb

   ____ transitive verb   ____ subject pronoun

   ____ noun used as a subject

Lesson #9

1. Place commas before and after the nonrestrictive phrase.

   Our dog excited to go on a walk wagged his tail enthusiastically.

2. Underline the simple subject and select the verb that agrees.

   Our Olympic swim team (practice / practices) every day.

   Mark Spitz and Michael Phelps (is / are) two of the greatest American swimmers in the history of the sport.

3. Read the sentences below. Identify the fragment and rewrite it as a complete sentence on the line.

   Our softball team made the playoffs. Our final game is on Saturday. Against Roosevelt, one of our fiercest rivalries. We're going to win!

   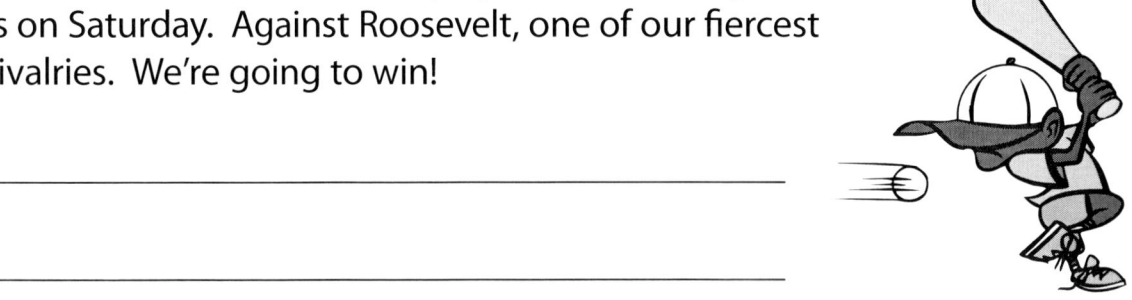

   _____

   _____

4. Complete the sentences using the past perfect form of the verb *challenge*.

   Liam _____ himself to swim fast enough to make the team.

   The teachers _____ the students with a spelling bee.

5. Match the correct spelling of each word with its definition.

isle	the passage between rows of seats
aisle	a small island

allowed	a verb meaning to permit
aloud	an adverb meaning speaking in a way that can be heard

6. **An effect is *what happened*; the cause tells *why it happened*.**

   Cause: Mahatma Gandhi believed *intolerance* toward those of other races, religions, or classes is a destructive force in a society.
   Effect: Followers of Gandhi strove to accept different cultures.

   From the cause/effect relationship, you can tell intolerance is _____.

   A) fairness   B) equality   C) lack of acceptance

7. Use a correlative conjunction pair that best completes the sentence.

   For game day, Theo brought _____ Scrabble and

   Backgammon _____ several decks of cards.

8. This email has five errors. Find and mark each error with a proofreading mark. A table of proofreading marks is in the *Help Pages*.

   I am interested in volunteering at the libary this Summer. I have experience babysitting dog sitting. My neighbors they think I am very reliable. I have a letter of recommendation from ms. Jeffers.

9. **Avoid using a pronoun if using it makes the sentence unclear.** Change one word to make the meaning of the sentence clear.

   I took an apple out of my lunchbox and put it away.

10. Underline the transitive verb in the sentence; double underline the direct object.

    The hungry brown bear swatted the hive of angry buzzing bees.

Lesson #10

1. Circle the object pronoun.

   As soon as our pizza was ready, it was served to us.

2. Choose the pronoun that agrees with the antecedent.

   Scientists are studying a colony of bats to learn about (their / its) habitat.

3. Choose a correlative conjunction pair that best completes the sentence.

   If Miguel hits _____ many homeruns _____ he did in practice, Washington Middle School will win the tournament.

4. Follow the spelling rules to add a suffix to each root.

   control + ed → _____   maintain + ing → _____

   propel + er → _____   occur + ence → _____

   feast + ed → _____   box + ing → _____

5. Write the missing verbs in the chart; assume the subject is *they*.

Present	Past	Present Progressive	Present Perfect
solve	A)	are solving	have solved
B)	dressed	C)	D)
carry	E)	are carrying	F)

6. Underline the adverb.

   We're catching the train tomorrow, so don't be late.

7. Use context clues to determine the meaning of *ambiguity*. Use a dictionary to verify the meaning.

   The politician's explanation did little to lessen the ambiguity of his position on the issue.

       importance   uncertainty   luxury   righteousness

8. **Use parentheses to insert a sentence that is not part of the flow of the writing.**

   Example: There is often an insufficient number of parent volunteers for the middle school field trip. (One year it was cancelled due to the lack of volunteers.) If you think you are able to volunteer, please see Mrs. Reynolds.

   Insert parentheses around extra information.

   Our family is vacationing at the seashore this summer. All of our younger cousins are coming. They've all had swimming lessons. We'll be staying in a cottage that is a short walk from the shore.

9. Choose the correct spelling of each word to complete the sentence.

   (There / They're) is not going to be enough snow to alpine ski.

   They brought (they're / their) cross country skis, just in case.

10. Read the sentences below. Identify the fragment and rewrite it as a complete sentence on the line.

    Can't wait for the sleepover at Chelsea's house. I packed snacks and video games. We are going to have a great time.

    _____

    _____

Lesson #11

1. Match each type of sentence to what it does.

    ____ asks something   A) declarative

    ____ tells something   B) exclamatory

    ____ gives a command   C) interrogative

    ____ shows strong feeling   D) imperative

2. Make one compound sentence from these two simple sentences.

    Margaret's team entered the jump rope competition. The event was rained out.

    _____

    _____

3. Choose the word with the more positive connotation in each sentence.

    We (envy / admire) Martine's blue ribbons in dressage.

    Wylie amassed a fortune being (thrifty / miserly).

4. The prefix *anti-* means "against or opposite"; the prefix *ante-* means "before." Write the letter that matches the word.

    ____ anticlimax   A) toward the front

    ____ anterior   B) disappointing ending

5. Underline the prepositional phrase and circle the preposition. Write the object of the preposition.

    The wind howled into our sails propelling us forward. _____

6. Insert the commas before and after a nonrestrictive phrase.

   All the girls *who are in the seventh grade* are required to take a gym class. One of the benefits of exercise *as everyone knows* is being physically fit.

7. The word *prejudice* is in the same category as the words *bigotry, intolerance,* and *discrimination.* Which is another word for *prejudice*?

   respect   bias   indifference   fairness

8. **A pronoun in the predicate of a sentence may be a predicate nominative.** A predicate nominative renames the subject.

   Example: The pastry chef is he.
   (*he* renames *chef*)

   Choose the correct pronoun in each sentence.

   The representative is (he / him). The last ones to board are (we / us).

9. Read the sentences below and identify the figure of speech in each.

   A) simile   B) metaphor

   _____ Manny had been on an *emotional roller coaster* for most of the summer.
   _____ The insult had *stung like a bee.*

10. What is being compared in the figures of speech in item 9?

    _____Manny's emotions_____ and _____

    _____ and _____

Lesson #12

1. Each word choice below has a slightly different connotation. Match the most appropriate word with each sentence.

   decrepit   The peeling paint made the new house look _____.

   shabby   My old house was so _____ I feared it would collapse.

   rickety   The wheel on my _____ bicycle wobbled when I rode it.

2. **Insert a comma before and after contrasting phrases within a sentence.**

   Example: Let's go to the art museum, not the zoo, on Friday.

   Underline the contrasting phrase. Insert two commas.

   I've decided to buy a poster of this Van Gogh landscape rather than his self-portrait with my savings.

3. Match each word with its clue.

   ____ stationery   A) not moving (adjective)

   ____ stationary   B) paper for letter-writing (noun)

4. Match each type of conjunction with its definition.

   ____ correlative   A) work in pairs to join words

   ____ coordinating   B) joins a dependent clause with a main clause

   ____ subordinating   C) joins a compound subject, compound predicate, or compound sentence

5. Underline the complete subject; double underline the simple subject.

   The movie that will be shown is an old Charlie Chaplin film.

6. Label the complete subject and the complete predicate in this simple sentence. Circle the simple predicate.

   High winds and large rolling waves   carried our beach umbrella out to sea.
                    A   B

   A) _____   B) _____

7. The simple sentence above has a compound (subject / predicate) joined by a (coordinating / subordinating) conjunction.

8. Draw a line through the fragment; rewrite it as a complete sentence.

   Tried on my new swimsuit. It was the wrong size. My mom packed it up and took it to the post office.

   _____

   _____

9. **A compound subject with two singular parts that are joined by *or* or *nor* uses a singular verb.**

   Example: Jon or Monica is spotting the gymnasts on the balance beam.

   Choose the correct verb.

   Neither Rachel nor Sissy (have / has) taken a turn on the parallel bars.

10. **When a part of the compound subject is plural, the verb is also plural, even when using the words *or* or *nor*.**

    Example: Neither the coach nor the gymnasts know when the meet begins.

    Choose the correct verb.

    The coach and the judges (have / has) the names of all competitors.

Lesson #13

1. Choose the correct spelling of each word to complete the sentence.

   (It's / Its) almost warm enough to go swimming. That turtle is out sunning (it's / its) shell on the back of that log.

2. **Sometimes a pronoun in the predicate of a sentence is a predicate nominative. A predicate nominative renames the subject using a subjective case pronoun.** Complete each sentence with a pronoun. Write O if it is an object pronoun or P if it is a predicate nominative.

   Margery asked _____ to help clean. I told her I'd gladly help. _____

   Everyone voted for Anthony. The new captain is _____. _____

   Alanna has her chauffeur's license. The driver will be _____. _____

   Star Song Records liked his voice. They gave _____ a contract. _____

3. Write each meaning next to the prefix or suffix it matches.

             time   without   half   study of

   -ology   zoology, hematology, lexicology _____

   chrono- chronicle, chronometer, chronic _____

   -less   restless, aimless, shapeless _____

4. Underline the complete predicate and double underline the simple predicate.

   Next Saturday, we will have soccer practice at the high school field.

5. Choose the correct pronouns.

   (Whose / Who's) turn is it to wash the dishes?

   (Whose / Who's) going to dry the dishes if I wash them?

6. **Parentheses and dashes can be used to frame a nonrestrictive phrase.**

    Examples: Margarite — my eldest sister — is home from college. She will graduate from Notre Dame — the Fighting Irish — in June.

    Place parentheses around the nonrestrictive element.

    School in case you haven't heard is on a two hour delay today.

7. Write the missing verbs in the chart using the subject *I*.

Present	Past	Past Progressive	Past Perfect
scurry	scurried	was scurrying	A)
map	B)	C)	had mapped
drive	D)	E)	F)

8. **A compound sentence is two or more simple sentences joined by a coordinating conjunction.** Underline each complete thought and add a comma.

    Jamie always remembers his lunch money but he forgot it today.

9. **In a complex sentence, a subordinating conjunction joins a thought that can stand alone with one that cannot.** Underline the complete thought; double underline the subordinate clause.

    Jenna would not lend Jamie lunch money unless he promised to pay her back tomorrow.

10. Circle the subordinating conjunction in the above item.

Lesson #14

1. Match each underlined pronoun with its type. Use each type once.

   ____ I gave <u>her</u> a dozen tulips.   A) possessive

   ____ The Olympic diver was <u>he</u>.   B) objective case

   ____ Adrienne lost <u>her</u> car keys.   C) predicate nominative

   ____ <u>They</u> are our new neighbors.   D) subjective case

2. The following sentence includes a metaphor. What two things does it compare?

   In the Peanuts comic strip by Charles M. Schulz, the character known as Pig Pen is a dirt magnet.

   _____ and _____

3. Match the correct spelling of each word with its definition.

   ____ waist   A) loss of something valuable through careless or unnecessary use

   ____ waste   B) narrowed middle part of a body or a garment

4. Choose the verbs that agree.

   A pack of wolves (is / are) thriving in Yellowstone National Park.

   This fleet of tall ships (sail / sails) from Portugal every July.

5. Choose a subordinating conjunction to complete the sentence.

         rather than   as if   even though

   Our book club will read this mystery for its next book _____ _____ there are no copies available at the library.

6. Choose the word with the appropriate connotation. Use each word once.

   A) aroma   B) smell   C) stench

   The _____ from the sewage treatment plant caused us hold our noses.

   I loved the _____ that came from my grandmother's kitchen whenever she cooked.

   Baking soda in the refrigerator keeps the _____ of strong foods from becoming overpowering.

7. What is the relationship between the first two words?

   tree : forest :: _____ : _____

   A) tree is the opposite of forest
   B) tree and forest are synonyms
   C) tree is part of a forest
   D) tree is a type of forest

8. Use the relationship in the previous item to decide the second part of the analogy. Which two words have the same relationship as tree and forest?

   automobile : car   flower : garden   scientist : experiment   ocean : fish

9. Giving animals or inanimate objects human characteristics is a figure of speech.

   What figure of speech is it? _____

   Write an example. _____

10. What is the subject of the following sentence?

    Open your books to page 125.   _____

Lesson #15

1. **Some indefinite pronouns are singular and take singular verbs and singular pronouns.**

   Examples: <u>Everyone</u> *pays* for *her* own ticket. <u>Neither</u> price *is* correct.

   Underline the indefinite pronoun. Complete each sentence with a possessive pronoun.

   No one is marked tardy if _____ bus is late. Someone will help you if you ask _____. Either of the dogs dog can get _____ bath now.

2. Complete each sentence using the designated form of the verb *think*.

   Cheyenne _____ about taking a trip to Thailand.
   (present progressive)

   Ron _____ the cat would get along with the new puppy.
   (past perfect)

3. Write the subject of the sentence on the line. Circle the sentence type.

   Remember to make a reservation.   _____

       declarative   interrogative   imperative   exclamatory

4. Cross out a vague word in this sentence; write a new word above to make the meaning clear.

   Eli and Al switched bikes because he wanted to try a road bike.

5. Cross out the incorrect form of the verb *be*; write the correct form above.

   She be the first one in line again.

   We was tired from last night's practice.

6. Circle the simple subject and select the verb that agrees. Underline the prepositional phrase.

   My neighbor along with his four dogs (visit /visits) the dog park every Saturday morning.

7. Underline the pronoun; circle its antecedent. Write I if it is an *intensive* pronoun and R if it is *reflexive*.

   _____ Chaz left himself just enough time to shower and dress.

   _____ The dog itself frightened away the burglars.

   _____ Sabrina thought herself lucky to be chosen.

8. Match each figure of speech with its definition.

   ____ simile

   ____ idiom

   ____ metaphor

   A) a comparison in which something is said *to be* something else

   B) a saying with a figurative — not literal — meaning

   C) a comparison in which something is said to be *like* or *as* something else

9. Use a subordinating conjunction to join these sentences. Write a complex sentence.

   Elijah wanted to go mountain biking. It looked like rain.

   _____

   _____

10. Look at the word *anthropomorphic*. Underline the part of the word that means *human* and circle the part that means *form*. What is the meaning the word *anthropomorphic*?

    anthropomorphic _____

Lesson #16

1. Underline each pronoun and circle its antecedent. Write R if the pronoun is *reflexive* or I if it is *intensive*.

   _____ We did all the work ourselves. _____ Jordan is fishing by himself.

2. The nouns have been underlined in each sentence. Write C above each common noun and P above each proper noun.

   Next <u>Friday</u>, <u>Independence</u>, <u>Ohio</u> is receiving an <u>award</u> from the <u>Environmental Protection Agency</u>. There will be a big <u>ceremony</u>.

3. Underline the prepositional phrase.

   Cara stared straight ahead throughout the lengthy program.

   Write the preposition. _____

   Write the object of the preposition. _____

4. Underline the simple subject. Choose the verb that agrees with the subject.

   A platter of colorfully-frosted treats (awaits / await) us.

5. Write the meaning of each prefix.

   circum– _____   hemi– _____

   micro– _____   neo– _____

6 – 7. Match each underlined pronoun with its type.

　　____ Sadie is <u>their</u> first kitten.　　A) possessive

　　____ <u>We</u> watched them disembark.　　B) objective case

　　____ Can you see <u>it</u>?　　C) predicate nominative

　　____ The former tenants are <u>they</u>.　　D) subjective case

8. Study the sentences.

   Cause: A non-native species invades a habitat where it has no predators.

   Effect: The invasive species disrupts food webs <u>decimating</u> native species.

   From the cause/effect relationship, you can tell *decimate* means to ____.

   　　rebuild　　greatly increase　　wipe out　　outlaw

9. Choose the word with an appropriate connotation to complete each sentence. Use each word once.

   　　A) invention　　B) discovery　　C) innovation

   A recent scientific _____ is the knowledge of which gene controls which human characteristic.

   Apple cellular technology usually has an outstanding _____ or two which makes consumers want to upgrade to a new phone.

   Lonnie G. Johnson, an African-American engineer and NASA scientist, is credited with the _____ of the world-famous Super Soaker squirt gun.

10. Complete the sentence with a plural indefinite pronoun and a possessive pronoun.

    _____ pack _____ own lunches.

Lesson #17

1. Write a C if the underlined part is a *cause* or an E if it is an *effect*.

   _____ <u>Chandler panicked</u> when the paint ran out before he had finished painting the wall.

   _____ Mateo volunteered to run to the hardware store <u>since Chandler couldn't finish without more paint</u>.

2. **These indefinite pronouns can be either singular or plural.**

   all   any   more   most   none   some

   Examples: <u>Most</u> of the doughnuts are chocolate.
   (*Most* refers to doughnuts, which is plural.)

   Most of the pizza is onion.
   (*Most* refers to pizza, which is singular.)

   Underline the indefinite pronoun. Write an S for singular or a P for plural above. Choose the verb that agrees.

   The tulips are blooming, but none (has / have) been picked yet.

   I filled all the vases with water, but most (has / have) evaporated.

3. Underline each independent clause; circle the subordinating conjunction.

   My mom will come and pick us up whenever we are ready.

   Even though Kimberly also needs a ride, our car is already full.

4. Use a dictionary to match each word's spelling with its clue.

   ____ lie   A) a verb meaning to put or set something down

   ____ lay   B) a verb meaning getting into a horizontal position

5. Cross out the incorrect verb; write a replacement above.

   We will need to wait for Olivia because she have our tickets.

6. Use a subordinating conjunction to join these sentences. Write a complex sentence.

   Ella insisted the twins help clean up. They had made the mess in the first place.

   _____

   _____

7. **The pronoun *who* is used as a subject; the pronoun *whom* is used as a direct object or the object of a preposition.** Choose the correct pronoun.

   For (who / whom) did you make the striped scarf?

   (Who / Whom) wants the last slice of cake?

8. *Whoever* **is a subject pronoun;** *whomever* **is an object pronoun.**

   Examples: Whoever left his keys here will probably return.
   (subject)

   Let's ride with whomever has room in her car.
   (object of a preposition)

   Choose the correct pronoun.

   (Whoever / Whomever) let the dog out should go and find him.

   Our shelter gives food to (whoever / whomever) is hungry.

9. Underline the metaphor in the following passage.

   I would not have gotten through sixth grade if it were not for my Aunt CeeCee. She is my fairy godmother.

10. What two things are being compared in the figure of speech?

    _____ and _____

Lesson #18

1. Substitute a noun for the vague pronoun.

   The bus rounded the corner leaving the
   city behind; soon we could no longer see it. _____

2. Complete each sentence using the designated form of the verb *invite*.

   I _____ everyone in my class to the party.
   　　　(present progressive)

   Ramona _____ over one hundred people.
   　　　　　(future perfect)

3. Add commas to set off the nonrestrictive phrases.

   The painting as you can see is a self-portrait of Vincent Van Gogh. His brush strokes normally bold and dramatic are clipped and calm in this self-portrait.

4. Read the sentence and look at the words that are underlined. Match each word with its function.

   <u>Someone</u> at the meeting <u>showed</u> the <u>mayor</u> a <u>pothole</u> <u>in</u> his <u>district</u>.
   　　A　　　　　　　　　　　　B　　　　　　C　　　　D　　E　　　F

   ____ transitive verb　　　　　____ direct object

   ____ indirect object　　　　　____ object of the preposition

   ____ preposition　　　　　　　____ indefinite pronoun

5. Choose the correct object pronouns.

   The photographer took lots of pictures of
   (we and them) / (them and us) / (we and they).

Summer Solutions©   Common Core English Grammar & Mechanics 6

6. Read the sentences below. Draw a line through the fragment and rewrite it as a complete sentence on the line.

   My grandparents are celebrating their golden anniversary in June. Everyone is coming to a big party to help them celebrate. All my cousins, aunts, uncles, and family friends.

   _____

   _____

7. Choose the verb that agrees with the collective noun.

   The platoon of soldiers (march / marches) toward the general.

8. The words *wild* and *energetic* both refer to an active state. Decide which word has the most appropriate connotation for each sentence, and fill it in below.

   wild: frantic, uncivilized, unrestrained   **energetic**: lively, active, brisk

   A) The audience howled like _____ animals until the band returned to the stage.

   B) The _____ performers were able to dance for hours.

9. Underline the reflexive or intensive pronoun; circle its antecedent. Write an I if it is an *intensive* pronoun and an R if it is *reflexive*.

   _____ We thought of ourselves as ready for any emergency.

   _____ They had not given themselves enough credit.

   _____ She carried the flag herself.

10. Find the word *abate* in a dictionary. Choose its meaning.

    A) a verb meaning the lessening of something negative or threatening
    B) a partial refund or pay back
    C) a noun meaning a discussion with many people

Lesson #19

1. Choose the best correlative conjunction pair to complete the sentence.

    Poppy is very, very cold; she is wearing _____ her hat with the big pom pom _____ her ear muffs.

2. What is the subject of each sentence?

    Please remember to let the dog out.   _____

    Jonathan will take the kettle off the stove.   _____

3. Insert commas as needed.

    We went to the dance not the movies last night.

    Armand won the 200 meter freestyle not the 200 meter backstroke.

4. Read the following sentence. Underline the figure of speech.

    One of the sport car's headlamps had been burned out for days. It had been winking flirtatiously at every oncoming car.

    The type of figurative language is _____.

5. **The interrogative pronoun *who* is used as a subject or a predicate nominative; it corresponds with the pronouns *he*, *she*, or *they*.**

    Example: Who is our governor?
    (Think: He is our governor.)

    Choose the correct pronouns.

    (Who / Whom) will be the next mayor of our city?

    The polls predict our next mayor will be (him / he).

6. Complete each sentence using the verb *create*.

   You can _____ a wildlife-friendly habitat in your yard.
   (simple present tense)

   Habitat destruction _____ a need for new habitats for
   (present perfect)

   many animals. Soon, many families _____
   (future perfect)

   wildlife-friendly habitats providing food, water, and shelter.

7. **Sometimes the subject of the sentence comes after the verb. Don't be fooled — the subject and verb must agree!**

   Example: One of the best science fiction films ever made is *Star Wars*.
                                                                  verb subject

   Choose the verb that agrees.

   Among my favorite summer reading books (are / is) *Catching Fire*.

8. Which type of sentence is this?

   Mom said I can go to New York City to visit Emily!

       declarative   interrogative   imperative   exclamatory

9. Add an intensive pronoun. Circle the antecedent in the sentence.

   She scored all the goals _____.

   They painted the fence _____.

10. Which word correctly completes the analogy?

    transports : train :: bakes : _____.

        chef   oven   casserole   eating

Lesson #20

1. Identify each type of sentence. Add the correct end punctuation.

   ____ declarative   A) Take the first downtown bus

   ____ exclamatory   B) Have you seen this film yet

   ____ imperative   C) I'm taking biology this semester

   ____ interrogative   D) I won a trip to Paris

2. **Some possessive pronouns are used with nouns. Other possessive pronouns can stand alone.**

   Examples: Here is *my* ballot. This ballot is <u>mine</u>.

   Choose one of these possessives to complete the sentences.

   Are those (your / yours) shoes? They look too big to be (your / yours).

   Anna paid for (her / hers) ticket, so this is (her / hers).

   Can you ride in (their / theirs) van? We don't have room in (our / ours).

3. Write the correct pronoun for each singular noun and underline the antecedent. Circle the verb that agrees.

   The navy regularly navigates ships through the channel; sailing is something _____ (do / does) very well.

   A flock of ducks paddles along. _____ (escort / escorts) the ships.

4. Underline the contrasting phrase. Insert two commas.

   I volunteered to feed the neighbor's dog not walk it while the neighbors are on vacation.

5. **A relative pronoun relates a group of words to the rest of the sentence.** Underline the relative pronoun and circle its antecedent.

   Example: The (team) *that came in last place* received new uniforms.

   My cousin *who lives in Detroit* is a big Tigers fan.

6. Match the correct spelling of each word with its *clue*.

affect	a noun meaning a change that is the result of an action
effect	a verb meaning to act on or have an impact
dissent	to disagree with an official position or set of beliefs
descent	the act or process of going down

7. Complete each sentence using the designated form of the verb *appear*.

   My favorite band _____ on stage soon. It
   (future progressive)

   _____ with a new singer only once before.
   (future perfect)

8. Rewrite these words with the suffixes.

   lobby + *ist* → _____   employ + *ment* → _____

   happy + *ness* → _____   reply + *ed* → _____

   baby + *ish* → _____   play + *able* → _____

9. Place parentheses around the nonrestrictive element.

   We're moving to Evanston outside of Chicago before school starts.

10. Choose the correct pronoun.

    The fastest runners are (she / her) and Dwight.

Lesson #21

1. Match each root or suffix with its meaning.

    ____ amphi   A) time

    ____ chrono   B) both

    ____ ante   C) before

2. Find and mark two errors in each sentence with a proofreading mark.

    Celestine lent me the book she received as a hanukkah gift

    Unfortuneately, I missed the picnic on the first day of Summer.

    Marlisa and I we could not wait to soccer.

3. Replace the underlined part with a pronoun.

    Kaley is bringing <u>Jordan and Meghan</u> their lunch.   _____

    <u>Clinton and I</u> are eating at this picnic table.   _____

    Deon's mom packed <u>Deon's</u> lunch because he is vegetarian.   _____

4. Underline the indefinite pronoun; choose the words that agree.

    Everyone could recall (his / their) first stuffed animal.

    Not all of the students could ski, but many (is / are) learning.

5. What do you think the word *insidious* means? Use a dictionary to verify the meaning.

    The practical jokes seemed harmless at first, but became more insidious with the passage of time.

           hilarious   reluctant   harmful   potent

6. Match each pronoun type with its example.

   reflexive   She dressed her baby brother, and then she fed herself.

   intensive   He carried the bike up three flights of stairs himself.

7. Read the sentences and look at the words that are underlined. Match each word with its function.

   I <u>already</u> <u>finished</u> <u>my</u> <u>homework</u>. <u>That</u> <u>was</u>
     A   B   C   D   E   F

   the first thing I did <u>when I got home</u>.
                             G

   ____ linking verb

   ____ transitive verb   ____ direct object

   ____ adverb   ____ possessive pronoun

   ____ adverb phrase   ____ demonstrative pronoun

8. Write a C if the underlined part is a *cause* or an E if it is an *effect*.

   ____ The slant of the earth's axis <u>determines which hemisphere is tilted towards the sun</u>.

   ____ <u>When a hemisphere is tilted towards the sun</u>, it experiences its summer season.

9. Cross out the vague pronoun; write a noun that makes the sentence clear.

   Sis and Ann switched hats because the red one did not match her coat. _____

10. Draw a line through the fragment. What is missing from the fragment?

             subject   verb   both

    Lily and I made pancakes for Sunday breakfast. Really delicious when covered in blueberry syrup. Dad ate a mountain of them.

Lesson #22

1. Add an intensive or reflexive pronoun and circle the antecedent. Write R if the pronoun is *reflexive* or I if it is *intensive*.

   _____ We called all the registered voters _____.

   _____ He gave _____ extra time to train the others.

2. **Avoid using a pronoun if there is no antecedent.**

   Not Clear: I met my mom where *they* told me she would be.
   Clear: I met my mom where *my cousins* told me she would be.

   Cross out the pronoun with no antecedent. Write some words above to make the sentence clear.

   We lined up outside the cafeteria like they told us.

3. Read the sentences and look at the words that are underlined. Match each word with its function.

   The <u>graceful</u> eagle <u>soared</u> <u>magnificently</u> <u>overhead</u>. I <u>sent</u> our
        A   B   C   D   E

   local <u>newspaper</u> the <u>pictures</u> <u>that</u> we took of the eagle on its nest.
           F   G   H

   ____ intransitive verb   ____ direct object

   ____ adverb that tells how   ____ adverb that tells where

   ____ relative pronoun   ____ adjective

   ____ transitive verb   ____ indirect object

4. What do you think the word *abstain* means? Use a dictionary to verify the meaning.

   The doctor recommended she <u>abstain</u> from eating sweets.

   A) brush her teeth afterward   C) not let sugar stain her clothing
   B) choose to not do something   D) eat sweets more often

5. Study the analogy.   cement mixer : truck : : spatula : utensil

   What can be said about the relationship between spatula and utensil?

   A) spatula and utensil are synonyms   C) spatula is part of a utensil
   B) spatula and utensil are antonyms   D) spatula is a type of utensil

6. Join these two sentences into one complex sentence.

   I crossed to the other side of the street. I was afraid of that barking dog.

   _____

   _____

7. Choose the correct pronoun.

   Sari told me (who / whom) is going on vacation next.

   We wondered with (who / whom) she would be traveling.

8. Insert commas before and after contrasting phrases.

   Let's eat a healthy salad not a pizza for dinner tonight.

   Let's stay in touch by email not just by text messages over the summer.

9. Write C above each *common* noun and P above each *proper* noun.

   Tom Hanks is the voice of Sheriff Woody in *Toy Story*, a film made by Pixar Animation Studios based in California.

10. Identify each sentence; write simple, compound or complex.

    _____ I ride my bike wherever there are marked lanes.

    _____ Jon and Laney swept the cabin free of spider webs.

Lesson #23

1. Read the following sentence. Underline the figure of speech.

   A delicious aroma floated out of the kitchen beckoning everyone to dinner with its long wispy fingers.

   The type of figurative language is _____.

2. Select the subject pronoun that acts as a predicate nominative.

   The volunteers for the river clean-up are (them / they).

3. Use a dictionary to match the correct spelling of each word with its definition.

   hoarse   a four-legged animal
   horse   describes a rough or harsh voice

   forth   an adverb meaning onward or forward
   fourth   a noun meaning the number four in a series

4. Spelling rules help establish patterns for spelling. Match each word with the rule that explains its formation.

   ____ study + *ous* → studious   A) Do not drop the final *e* when a suffix begins with a consonant.

   ____ arrange + *ment* → arrangement   B) Change the *y* to *i* before adding a suffix when a consonant precedes the *y*.

5. Choose the correct pronoun.

   I will vote for (whoever / whomever) has the best ideas.

   (Whoever / Whomever) runs for council must be a resident.

6. Complete the chart; the subject is *we*.

	Past Perfect	Present Perfect	Future Perfect
lay			
forgive		have forgiven	
bit			

7. Choose the verb that agrees.

    In several tall piles next to my bed (is / are) my comic book collection.

8. Underline the prepositional phrases; circle the prepositions. Draw a rectangle around each object of the preposition.

    The skaters twirled on the ice for a minute between each performance.

    The Canadian pair earned perfect tens in each event except ice dancing.

9. Circle the verbs that agree in the sentences below. Write the correct pronoun on the line; circle the antecedent.

    I watch the colony of bats (exit / exits) the cave. _____ heads up into the mountains in search of mosquito delicacies and the like.

    Clearly the mosquitoes (sense / senses) the immediate danger. _____ suddenly stopped feasting on my exposed ankles and wrists.

10. Both *assertive* and *pushy* mean "forceful." *Assertive* connotes "confidence" whereas *pushy* implies "annoying." Fill in the word with the most appropriate connotation for each sentence.

    A) Don't be so _____ ; it is impolite to go out of turn.
    B) Our cause is important, so be _____ when you speak.

Lesson #24

1. The word pairs below have similar meanings but different connotations. Sort the words into two groups and list them in the graphic organizer.

   challenging / difficult   sneer / grimace

   distinctive / peculiar   envy / admire

Positive or Neutral	Negative

2. According to what you know about roots and suffixes, the word *bibliophile* probably means what?

   A) the story of a person's life
   B) electricity generated by lightning
   C) a person who loves or collects books
   D) list of websites

3. Join two sentences by writing a compound sentence.

   Chromosomes carry the genetic material. Chromosomes are located in the nucleus of a cell.

   _____

   _____

4. Write a C if the underlined part is a *cause* or E if it is an *effect*.

   _____ Because Lewis and Clark wrote about nature in the West, scientists learned about new plants and animals.

   _____ Lewis and Clark's expedition triggered a period of expansion which, in turn, led to the settling of the western frontier.

5. Underline the pronoun that correctly completes the sentence.

   They are holding the bus for Regina and (I / me).

   The only one who jumps off the high dive is (her / she).

   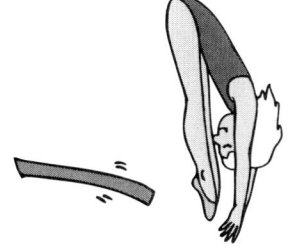

6. Underline each intensive pronoun; circle its antecedent.

   The babies themselves picked the pictures of their mothers.

   The coach himself selected the most valuable players.

7. Insert commas before and after contrasting phrases.

   I use walnuts never pecans in my secret recipe brownies.

   Grandma gives me a check not a present for my birthday each year.

8. Choose the word that best completes the analogy.

   pages : book :: bricks : _____

   bricklayer   stone   chimney   opera

9. Complete the sentences with the present perfect form of the verb *win*.

   Our school band _____ many awards. The percussionists _____ special honors every year of the competition.

10. Add the correlative conjunction pair that best completes the sentence.

    It is not too early to decide _____ you will go into the Peace Corps after high school _____ after college.

Lesson #25

1. Choose the correct pronoun for each sentence; circle the antecedent.

    Each governor tries to protect the interests of (his / their) state.

    I can see the herd of elk from here and (it is / they are) charging.

    Butterflies by the hundreds (emerge / emerges) from their chrysalides and take flight.

2. Cross out the vague pronoun. Write a noun above to make the sentence clear.

    The little puppy tired of fetching the ball, so I picked it up.

3. Write the forms of the irregular verbs if the subject is *I*.

	Past Perfect	Present Perfect	Future Perfect
eat			
deal			
swim			

4. Underline the simple subject and choose the correct verb.

    The jeans in the department store (is / are) going on sale this weekend.

    Ava's red hat, which matches her mittens, (is / are) on the top of the snowman's head now.

5. Cross out the vague pronoun. Write a word above to make the sentence clear.

    Nicolas tattled on Alfonso and now he is in trouble.

6. Draw a line through the fragment; rewrite it as a complete sentence.

   John Adams and Thomas Jefferson ran for president. Since John Adams received the most votes he became president, and Thomas Jefferson became vice president. Received the second highest number of votes.

   _____

   _____

7. An *outspoken* person is direct, honest, and open. A person who is *blunt* is also direct, but in a way that may be harsh or abrupt. In which sentence below is the speaker *blunt*?

   _____ You are a couch potato; you need to get up and start exercising.

   _____ I believe you will feel better if you get daily exercise.

8. Complete the sentence by adding the underline{future perfect form} of the verb *teach*.

   By the end of July you _____ yourself how to paint.

9. Choose the correct pronoun. Write O if it is an *object* pronoun or S if it is a *subject* pronoun.

   (She / Her) will hold our place in line.   _____

   (Who / Whom) wants to ride the Screamer with me?   _____

10. Use what you know about roots to match these words and meanings.

    ____ cuts across   A) thermal

    ____ sounds the same   B) diagonal

    ____ keeps you warm   C) homophone

Lesson #26

1. Identify each underlined pronoun.

   <u>He</u> donated <u>his</u> bike to <u>their</u> favorite charity. The person who accepted
    A   B   C

   the package was <u>she</u>. <u>We</u> donated to <u>them</u> last year.
                    D   E   F

   ____ singular subject pronoun   ____ object pronoun

   ____ plural subject pronoun   ____ predicate nominative

   ____ plural possessive pronoun   ____ singular possessive pronoun

2. Read each sentence below. Identify each sentence type.

         A) simple   B) compound   C) complex

   ____ Mason started reading my book, but he never finished it.

   ____ Cam practiced his cello and his viola whenever he had the time.

   ____ Jackson joined a bicycle club to ride with a group.

3. Underline the personification in the sentence below.

   The deer hungrily awaited the arrival of spring, but winter only tightened its stranglehold on the forest.

   What is given a human quality? _____

4. Study the analogy.   encourage : strengthen : : hinder : thwart

   Think about the relationship between *encourage* and *strengthen*.

   You can tell that *thwart* means _____.

          boost   prevent   make happy   assist

5. What is the subject of the sentence below? _____

   Come straight home from school today.

6. Study the word *autobiography*. Underline the part that means *written*, double underline the part that means *self*, and circle the part that means *life*. What does the word mean?

   autobiography   _____

7. Spelling rules help establish patterns for spelling. Match each word with the rule that explains its formation.

   ____ flip + *ing* → flipping   A) If the word has only one syllable or is accented on the last syllable and ends in a vowel + consonant pattern, double the final consonant.

   ____ carry + *er* → carrier   B) When adding a suffix to a word that ends in a consonant and *y*, change the *y* to *i*.

8. Choose the verb that agrees with the subject.

   Neither ice skating nor hockey (is / are) of interest to me.

   Both soccer and cycling (is / are) the sports I enjoy.

9. Write R if the underlined pronoun is *reflexive* or I if it is *intensive*.

   _____ Kim-Ly and Hao wrote their marriage vows <u>themselves</u>.

   _____ The sign said we can help <u>ourselves</u>.

10. Cross out the vague pronoun; write a noun below that makes the sentence clear.

    I banged my helmet when I crashed my bike, but it is fine.

Lesson #27

1. The verbs in each of the following sentences do not agree. Cross out one of the verbs and write the correct verb above it.

   Lydia saves her money for months, and she bought a new bicycle with it.

   She hoped to enter some races and begins training every day.

2. Complete the sentences with the <u>future progressive</u> form of the verbs.

   Marcus (will be feeding / will feed) the dogs while Sam is ill.

   Noah and I (are going / will be going) to visit him in the hospital.

3. Complete the sentence with the form of the verb *train*.

   Willem _____ for the Tour de France for many months.
   (present perfect)

   He _____ in the mountains of France once before.
   (past perfect)

   By the time Willem begins the race, he _____
   (future perfect)
   with some of the best cyclists in the world.

4. Choose the correct subject or object interrogative pronouns.

   (What / Which) time does the post office close?

   When you called the school, to (whom / who) did you speak?

   (Whose / Who's) car is parked in the principal's spot?

5. Choose the correct pronoun.

   (He / Him) and his dad go golfing together.

6. Use a dictionary to match the correct spelling of each word with its definition.

   pour   (verb) to read or study carefully and attentively
   pore   (verb) to make (a liquid or granular solid) stream or flow

   hole   (adjective) having all the parts; not divided
   whole   (noun) an opening; a pit dug in the ground

7. Add a reflexive or intensive pronoun; circle the antecedent. Write an I if it is *intensive* and an R if it is *reflexive*.

   _____   The cheerleaders bought _____ new pom poms.

   _____   She voted for _____.

   _____   We saw it _____.

8. Insert commas before and after contrasting phrases.

   I really liked driving the hybrid car not the gas-guzzler to the beach.

   Kenton wants to mow the lawn not weed the garden this week.

9. *Criticize* can mean "to find fault" or "to judge harshly." *Critique* means "to review" or "to analyze." Decide which word has the most appropriate connotation for the sentence below.

   The assignment was to read a novel and (critique / criticize) it.

10. Which website title is written correctly?

    _____   Tech Creation Learning Tools For Kids

    _____   *Tech Creation Learning Tools for Kids*

    _____   Tech creation learning tools for Kids

    _____   Tech Creation Learning Tools for Kids

Lesson #28

1. Insert commas as needed in the following sentences.

   You probably know since you rode to school with her that Grace's paintings were chosen for the community exhibit.

   No she didn't mention it.

2. Correct the verb error in the sentence below.

   They are going to the Empire State Building, and

   they wanted to buy their tickets.

3. Draw a line through the fragment; rewrite it as a complete sentence on the line.

   Explorer Hernando Cortes was welcomed by the Aztecs. Soon Cortes turned against the Aztecs and imprisoned their king. Successfully drove out the Spaniards.

   _____

   _____

4. Fill in verbs that agree with the subjects of these sentences.

       is   are   was   were

   Flowers, trees, and other flora _____ able to produce their own food using a process called photosynthesis.

   Neither Gregor Mendel nor other scientists of his day _____ sure how photosynthesis worked.

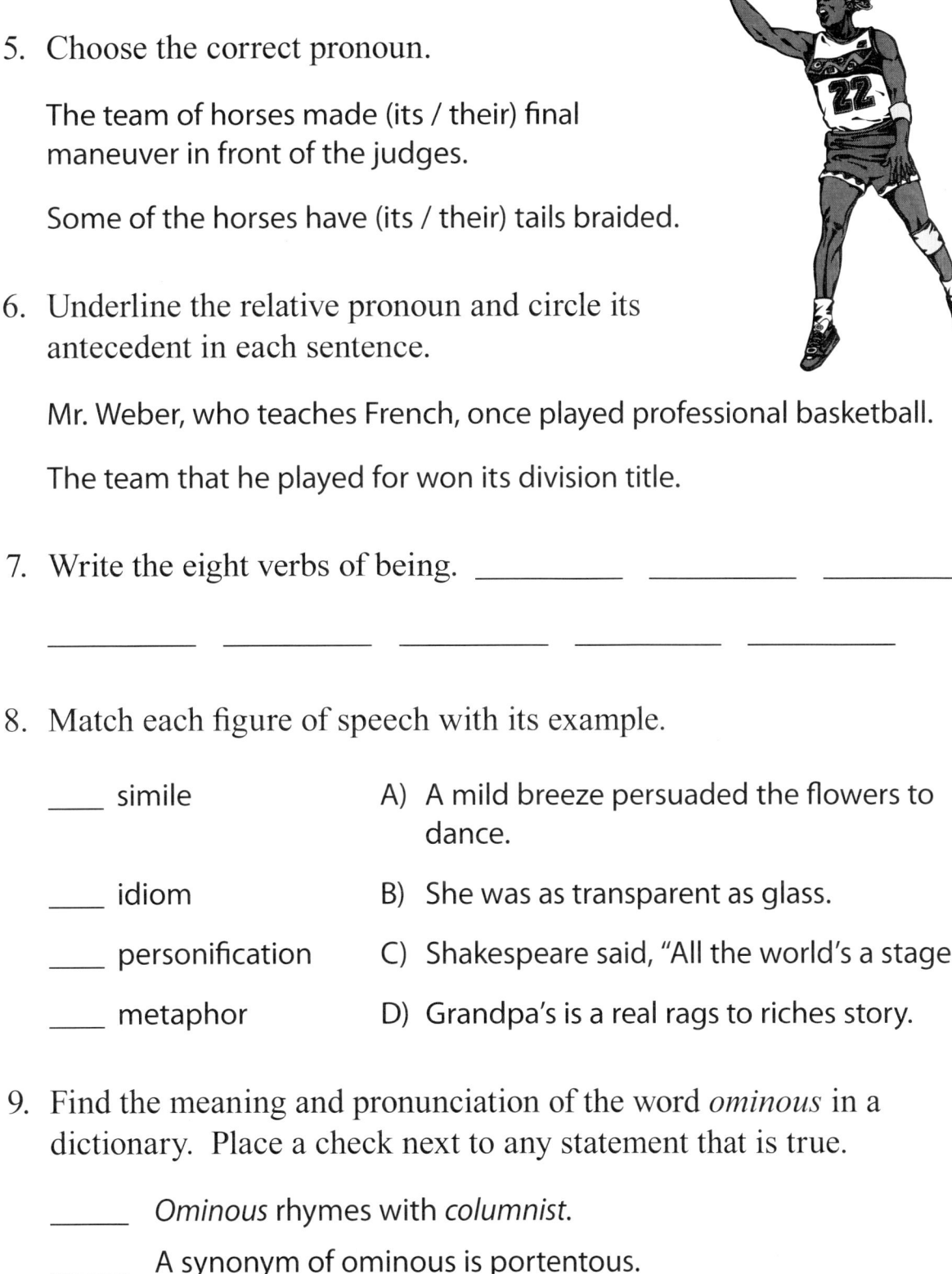

5. Choose the correct pronoun.

   The team of horses made (its / their) final maneuver in front of the judges.

   Some of the horses have (its / their) tails braided.

6. Underline the relative pronoun and circle its antecedent in each sentence.

   Mr. Weber, who teaches French, once played professional basketball.

   The team that he played for won its division title.

7. Write the eight verbs of being. _____ _____ _____

   _____ _____ _____ _____ _____

8. Match each figure of speech with its example.

   ____ simile   A) A mild breeze persuaded the flowers to dance.

   ____ idiom   B) She was as transparent as glass.

   ____ personification C) Shakespeare said, "All the world's a stage."

   ____ metaphor   D) Grandpa's is a real rags to riches story.

9. Find the meaning and pronunciation of the word *ominous* in a dictionary. Place a check next to any statement that is true.

   _____ *Ominous* rhymes with *columnist*.

   _____ A synonym of ominous is portentous.

   _____ *Ominous* means menacing.

10. What part of speech is the word *ominous*? _____

Lesson #29

1. Match each word to its clue.

   anachronism   opposition to war

   antiwar   an animal with a part land and part water lifecycle

   amphibian   something that belongs in a different time

2. Add a subordinating conjunction to complete each sentence.

   The Green Team and its advisor plan clean-up events _____ there is a need.

   _____ there was a torrential downpour, the students did not meet to clean up the creek or the shoreline.

3 – 4. Identify the function of each underlined word.

   The <u>sailboat</u> <u>listed</u> starboard as it glided <u>into</u> the <u>cove</u>. <u>It's</u> lucky
       A   B   C   D   E

   everyone <u>is</u> safe, except the boat <u>itself</u>; <u>its</u> sails were in tatters.
           F   G   H

   ____ contraction of *it* and *is*   ____ object of the preposition

   ____ preposition   ____ intensive pronoun

   ____ linking verb   ____ intransitive verb

   ____ singular possessive pronoun   ____ compound noun

5. Complete the sentence by adding the requested form of the verb *finish*.

   They _____ dinner when a stranger knocked at the door.
         (past progressive)

   They _____ dinner when a stranger knocked at the door.
         (past perfect)

6. Choose the correct subject or object interrogative pronouns.

   (What / Which) train goes to the ice rink?

   (What / Which) is the phone number for the pizzeria?

   For (who / whom) did you deliver all those flowers?

7. Cross out the vague pronoun: write a word above that makes the sentence's meaning clear.

   Emily and Meredith both live in New York City now, but she's moving to Rochester soon.

8. Write a complex sentence by joining an independent clause with a dependent clause. Use a subordinating conjunction.

   the Maya were able to develop the concept of zero

   they were capable mathematicians

   _____

   _____

9. Underline the intensive or reflexive pronoun. Circle its antecedent. Write I if it is an *intensive* pronoun or R if it is *reflexive*.

   _____ You better watch yourselves or you may fall.

   _____ Megan prepared the Thanksgiving dinner herself.

   _____ They momentarily forgot themselves and giggled raucously.

10. Write an indefinite pronoun that agrees with the verb.

    Everybody want to win the lottery. _____

    Many goes on vacation in
    July when the factory closes. _____

Lesson #30

1. Match each root or suffix with its meaning.

   ____ dia   A) take away

   ____ de   B) between

   ____ anti   C) against

   ____ inter   D) across

2. Use proofreader's symbols to show where the sentences should begin and end.

   We dove into the icy water to snorkel with our fins and masks we saw sand dollars and sea urchins in the shallows below if we held our breath we could dive down and look more closely.

3 – 4. Identify each part of speech and/or its function in the sentence. One choice will not be used.

   Look! Debris is bobbing everywhere in the current. Let's
     A   B   C   D

   show the lifeguard the debris.
    E   F   G

   ____ adverb   ____ direct object

   ____ indirect object   ____ preposition

   ____ object of the preposition   ____ transitive verb

   ____ intransitive verb   ____ interjection

5. Study the analogy.   panic : alarm : : contrite : apologetic

   Based on the analogy, choose the meaning of *contrite*.

   A) a synonym for *panic*   C) an antonym for *panic*
   B) a synonym for *apologetic*   D) an antonym for *apologetic*

6. Choose the correct pronouns.

   The coaches give (us / we) players too many laps to run!

   (We / Us) tennis players need to practice backhand shots.

7. Place a check next to each example of personification.

   _____ Anna giggled with her new friends.
   _____ The rusty old engine coughed and sputtered.
   _____ A full harvest moon peeked from behind the clouds.
   _____ The brittle brown leaves fell to the ground.

8. Choose the correct pronoun for the sentence.   its   their

   Neither the ferret nor the birds have had _____ cage cleaned.

9. Write the word with the appropriate connotation for each sentence.

           tricked   cheated

   A) On April Fool's Day, our teachers _____ us by mixing up the class schedule.

   B) The players felt _____ because the rain ended the game before they had a chance to tie up the score.

10. Underline the pronoun; write I if it is *intensive* and R if it is *reflexive*. Write its antecedent on the line.

    _____ They made themselves comfortable, but too soon it was time to start moving. _____

    _____ The boy with chicken pox looked at himself in the mirror and didn't recognize the face. _____

    _____ We ate the whole cake ourselves. _____

Common Core ENGLISH GRAMMAR & Mechanics 6

Help Pages

Some material addressed in standards covered at earlier grade levels may not be available in these *Help Pages*, but you can access all grade levels of *Simple Solutions Common Core English Grammar & Mechanics Help Pages* at SimpleSolutions.org.

Help Pages

Parts of Speech

There are eight parts of speech. The parts of speech are **nouns**, **pronouns**, **verbs**, **adverbs**, **conjunctions**, **adjectives**, **prepositions,** and **interjections**.

A word's **part of speech** is based on how it is used in a sentence. For example, a word is a noun if it functions as a subject, an object, or a predicate nominative.

Here are some examples of how the word *right* can be different parts of speech.

We respect your **right** to speak.	(noun—direct object)
Is this the **right** way?	(adjective)
These changes will **right** a wrong.	(verb)
My house is **right** next to the school.	(adverb)
Right! I absolutely agree.	(interjection)

Parts of Speech - Nouns

A **common noun** names a person, place, thing, or idea. Nouns may be singular or plural. A **proper noun** names a particular person, place, or thing. A proper noun begins with a capital letter.

Some of the Functions of Nouns

Subject — The subject is whom or what the sentence is about.
Example: Tom likes to play piano.

Direct Object — A direct object receives the action of the verb.
Example: Tom plays the piano.
To find the DO ask: Tom plays what? Tom plays the piano.

Indirect Object — An indirect object occurs only when there is a direct object.
Example: Mr. Gore gave the class an assignment.
Ask: To whom or for whom is the action of the verb directed?

Object of a Preposition — The object of a preposition comes at the end of a prepositional phrase.
Example: Mr. Gore plays in an orchestra.

Predicate Nominative (Predicate Noun) — A predicate nominative renames the subject.
Example: Tom and Mr. Gore are musicians.

Possessive — A possessive noun shows ownership and usually modifies another noun.
Example: Mr. Gore's class uses Tom's piano.

Parts of Speech - Pronouns

A **pronoun** takes the place of a noun. The noun that the pronoun is referring to is called the **antecedent**. The antecedent is in the same sentence or a recent earlier sentence; occasionally, an antecedent is not specifically named, it is implied, or "understood."

Examples: The puppy is in its pen.
(Puppy is the antecedent, so we know "its pen" means the puppy's pen.)
It has been raining all day.
(There is no clear antecedent, but we know "it" refers to the weather.)

Help Pages

Types of Pronouns

Case	Personal Pronouns
Subjective	Used as the subject of a sentence or clause
	Singular: I, you, he/she, it
	Plural: we, you, they
Objective	Used as an object; found in the predicate of a sentence
	Singular: me, you, him/her, it
	Plural: us, you, them
Possessive	Used to show ownership; modify nouns
	Singular: my, mine*, your, yours*, his*, her, hers*, its*
	Plural: our, ours*, your, yours*, their, theirs*
	* These can stand alone.

Other Types of Pronouns

Indefinite	Replaces a noun that is not specific
	Singular: another, anybody, anyone, anything, each, either, everybody, everyone, everything, little, much, neither, nobody, no one, nothing, one, other, somebody, someone, something
	Plural: both, few, many, others, several
	Either: all, any, more, most, none, some
Relative	Relates a group of words to the rest of the sentence
	(that, which, who, whose, whom, whoever, whomever, whichever, whatever)
Interrogative	Asks a question
	(what, which, who, whom, whose)
Demonstrative	Points out a noun or acts as an adjective
	(this, that, these, those)
Reflexive	Refers back to the subject
	Singular: myself, yourself, himself, herself, itself
	Plural: ourselves, yourselves, themselves
Intensive	Emphasizes a noun
	Singular: myself, yourself, himself, herself, itself
	Plural: ourselves, yourselves, themselves

Help Pages

Notes on Pronouns

Interrogative pronouns ask a question (What? Which? Who?). *Whom* is the objective case of *who*, and *whose* is the possessive of *who*.

Use the pronoun *who* as a subject or predicate nominative just like other nominative case pronouns (he, she, or they).

Example: **Who** is your best friend? (*Who* is the subject of the sentence.)

Use the pronoun *whom* as an object just like other objective case pronouns (him, her, or them).

Example: For **whom** did you bake the cake? (*Whom* is the object of the preposition *for*.)

Use the pronoun *whose* to show possession just like other possessive pronouns (his, her, or their).

Example: Please call the children **whose** parents have arrived.

Demonstratives can act as pronouns or adjectives. As a pronoun, a demonstrative points out a noun. As an adjective, a demonstrative modifies a noun.

Examples: That is my house. (used as a pronoun)
Those flowers are red. (used as an adjective)

A **reflexive pronoun** refers back to the subject. A reflexive pronoun cannot be removed without changing the meaning of the sentence.

Example: Mindy e-mailed herself a copy of the recipe. vs. Mindy e-mailed a copy of the recipe.
A reflexive pronoun always refers to an antecedent, which in this case, is Mindy.

Intensive pronouns are the same as reflexive pronouns but are used differently. An intensive pronoun emphasizes its antecedent, and can be removed from a sentence without changing the meaning.

Example: Doris built the house herself. Doris built the house.

Parts of Speech - Verbs

Action (Transitive)	Send action to a direct object *Example*: A stunt man performs dangerous feats. (verb – performs, direct object – feats)
Action (Intransitive)	Have no direct object *Example*: The symphony performs every Sunday. (verb – performs, no direct object)
Being	Do not show action; show a state of being *Examples*: is, are, was, were, be, am, being, been
Linking	Links the subject with a noun or adjective *Examples*: appear, become, feel, seem, smell, taste, sounds, and all forms of *be*.
Auxiliary (Helping)	Used with a main verb to form a verb phrase *Examples*: is, are, was, were, be, am, being, been, might, could, should, would, can, do, does, did, may, must, will, shall, have, has, had

Help Pages

Verb Tense

Verb Tense tells the time when the action or condition of the verb occurs.

Simple Verb Tenses

Present	The action is occuring now or is unchanging.	The house is new. (singular subject) The boys swim. (plural)
Past	The action was started and completed in the past.	The clock stopped. (singular subject) The buses ran. (plural)
Future	The action will not start until the future.	The snow will fall. (singular subject) The lakes will freeze. (plural)

Perfect Verb Tenses

A **perfect verb tense** or **perfect verb form** describes a completed action. All perfect verb forms use past tense verbs.

Present (has / have)	Action is ongoing or indefinite.	Nick has finished two of his assignments. We have played soccer for five years.
Past (had)	Shows which event in the past happened first.	She had asked for help before she began working. The children had napped before coming down to dinner.
Future (will have)	Action will occur in the future, before some other action.	I will have completed my chores by bedtime. They will have learned the routines by next year.

Progressive Verb Tenses

A main verb that ends in *–ing* works with a helping verb to form the progressive tense. The verb phrase shows action that is ongoing in present, past, or future.

Present We are talking. **Past** We were talking. **Future** We will be talking.

Irregular Verbs

Irregular Verbs do not follow the patterns of simple or perfect tense. Such verbs must be memorized. Here is a list of some common irregular verbs.

Present	Past	Use with *has, have,* or *had*	Present	Past	Use with *has, have,* or *had*
bear	bore	born	hold	held	held
bite	bit	bitten	lie	lay	lain
bleed	bled	bled	light	lit / lighted	lit / lighted
buy	bought	bought	sing	sang	sung
cling	clung	clung	shine	shone	shone
deal	dealt	dealt	sit	sat	sat
feel	felt	felt	sleep	slept	slept
forgive	forgave	forgiven	spin	spun	spun
grind	ground	ground	string	strung	strung
hear	heard	heard	swim	swam	swum

Help Pages

Parts of Speech - Adverbs

Adverbs modify verbs, adjectives and other adverbs.

Adverbs That Tell *When*

after	earlier	last	now	seldom	then	when
afterwards	early	late	occasionally	since	today	whenever
again	finally	later	often	sometimes	tomorrow	while
always	first	never	once	soon	until	yesterday
before	frequently	next	permanently	still	usually	yet

Adverbs That Tell *How*

angrily	firmly	happily	noisily	quickly	selfishly	unbelievably
calmly	gracefully	kindly	perfectly	quietly	slowly	wildly
eagerly	greedily	loudly	politely	sadly	softly	willingly

Adverbs That Tell *Where*

downstairs	forward	inside	somewhere
far	here	outside	upstairs

Adverbs That Tell *To What Extent*

almost	completely	permanently	really	too
also	extremely	quite	scarcely	vaguely
barely	more	rather	thoroughly	very

Parts of Speech - Conjunctions

Conjunctions connect similar words, clauses, or phrases within a sentence.

Coordinating   Join two equal elements or two complete thoughts
(Use the acronym FANBOYS: *for, and, nor, but, or, yet, so.*)
Example: We swam in the ocean <u>and</u> roasted hot dogs over the fire.

Correlative   Work in pairs to join words
either/or   neither/nor   both/and   whether/or   as/as   if/then
Example: <u>Neither</u> Jim <u>nor</u> his father cared for mushrooms.

Subordinating   Join a complete thought with an incomplete thought
See chart below.
Example: Finish your homework <u>before</u> you go outside.

Examples of Subordinating Conjunctions

after	before	if	though	when
although	even if	since	till	whenever
as	even though	than	unless	wherever
because	how	that	until	while

Help Pages

Parts of Speech – Adjectives

Adjectives modify nouns or pronouns. Adjectives tell *how many*, *what color*, *how big*, *how small*, *what kind*, and so on. **Example**: He was a tall man.

A proper adjective begins with a capital letter. **Example**: Alaskan Husky.

An article is a special type of adjective (a, an, the). **Example**: Throw Jack the ball.

Parts of Speech – Prepositions

Prepositions relate nouns or pronouns to other words in the sentence. A **prepositional phrase** begins with a preposition and ends with a noun or a pronoun.

Some Common Prepositions

about	around	by	into	out	under
above	before	down	near	outside	underneath
across	behind	during	nearby	over	until
after	below	except	next to	past	up
against	beneath	for	of	through	upon
along	beside	from	off	throughout	with

Parts of Speech – Interjections

An interjection is a word or a phrase that shows emotion (surprise, relief, fear, or anger).
Examples: Ouch! Good grief! Wow!

Sentences

Features of a sentence
1. Begins with a capital letter
2. Ends with punctuation/end mark
3. Conveys a complete thought

Fragments
A fragment is not a sentence because it does not express a complete thought. A fragment is missing either a subject or a verb.

Examples: The book that I read. (missing a verb)   Running down the street. (missing a subject)

Run-on Sentences
A run-on is two or more complete thoughts that run together without proper punctuation or conjunctions.

Examples:

Incorrect: Lori wants to be a biologist because she likes nature but she does not enjoy being outside if it is cold because she is more of a warm weather person and some biologists must do research outside so maybe Lori should study something else instead.

Correct: Lori wants to be a biologist because she likes nature. However, Lori does not enjoy being outside if it is cold. She is more of a warm weather person and some biologists must do research outside. Maybe Lori should study something else instead.

Help Pages

Parts of a Sentence

Subject The **simple subject** has no modifiers. Every sentence has a simple subject.

The **complete subject** includes the simple subject plus all of the modifiers that go with it.

Example: A few ravenous **teenagers** devoured the pizza. *Teenagers* is the simple subject. *A few ravenous teenagers* is the complete subject.

Predicate The **simple predicate** is the verb.

The **complete predicate** is the verb as well as all the words that modify the verb.

Example: The tired children **climbed** slowly upstairs. *Climbed* is the simple predicate, or verb. *Climbed slowly upstairs* is the complete predicate.

The Four Sentence Types

Type	Other Name	Punctuation	Example:
declarative	statement	period	This is a sentence.
interrogative	question	question mark	Is this correct?
imperative	command/request	period	Please open the door.
exclamatory	exclamation	exclamation point	This is awesome!

Sentence Structure

Simple Parts: one complete thought; subject and predicate only
Example: We will hold a rally at the local park.

Compound Parts: two or more complete thoughts
Joined by: coordinating conjunction
Example: There will be speeches in the morning, and we will play games in the afternoon.

Complex Parts: join a complete thought with one or more incomplete thoughts
Joined by: subordinating conjunction
Example: The rally will last until dusk unless the weather is severe.

Restrictive and Nonrestrictive phrases

If a word or phrase is **nonrestrictive**, it can be removed without changing the meaning of the sentence. *Example*: Chocolate, *of course*, is the best ice cream flavor.

If a phrase is **restrictive**, you cannot remove it without changing the meaning of the sentence.
Example: The shop *around the corner* sells single slices of pizza.

Help Pages

	Punctuation
Dash (–)	Use a dash to set off extra information that comes in the middle or at the end of a sentence. This information is not essential to the meaning of the sentence. A dash can be used in the same way as a colon. Dashes are used for special effect and should not be used very often. ***Example:*** Dan Kick – a college all-star – is our new coach.
Semicolon (;)	Use a semicolon to separate items in a series if there are already commas in the items. ***Example***: Lorain, Ohio; New Castle, Pennsylvania; and Chicago, Illinois
Comma (,)	Use commas to separate words or phrases in a series. ***Example***: Sun brought a coloring book, some crayons, a pair of scissors, and a ruler.
	Use a comma to separate two independent clauses joined by a conjunction. ***Example***: Dad works in the city, and he is a commuter.
	Use a comma after an introductory word, such as an interjection. ***Example***: Hey, who wants to play tennis? Do not use a comma if there is an end mark after the interjection. ***Example***: Oh no! It's starting to rain.
	Use a comma to separate two words or two numbers when writing a date. ***Example***: Friday, April 8, 2011
	Use a comma between the city and state in an address. ***Examples***: Boston, MA Seattle, WA Honolulu, Hawaii
	Use a comma before or after a quote if there is no end mark. ***Example***: "You know," said Marta, "Robert is an excellent violinist."
	Insert a comma after introductory words or phrases in a sentence. ***Example***: On the other hand, you may not need any help.
	Use commas before and after "interrupting phrases" within a sentence. ***Example***: Ms. Cole, *the bank teller*, was very helpful.
	Use commas before and/or after contrasting phrases that use *not*. ***Example***: I worked on my science project, *not my essay*, all evening.
	Use a comma to separate the words *yes* and *no* from the rest of a sentence. ***Examples***: Yes, I will join you. No, thank you.
	Use a comma to separate a "tag question" from the rest of a sentence. ***Examples***: You saw that, didn't you? George will lead the choir, won't he?
	Use a comma to show direct address. ***Examples***: Please sit down, Mrs. Schumacher. Come here, Peggy, I want you to meet Mrs. Schumacher.
Apostrophe (')	Use an apostrophe to form contractions or to form a possessive noun. ***Examples***: I don't want to go. That was Sherry's little sister.

Help Pages

Punctuation (continued) - Other Types of Punctuation

Punctuating nonrestrictive elements: Use commas, parentheses, or dashes to separate nonrestrictive elements.

commas: Jerry, *as you may know*, is Coretta's brother. I will, *therefore*, call Jerry to get Coretta's address. *On the other hand*, I can look up the information myself.

parentheses: Poppy's Pizza Shop (in Wexford Plaza) won the award for best veggie pizza.
All of my sisters (including Vera) will be bridesmaids.

dashes: *The Sound of Music*—one of my favorite films—featured the music of Rogers and Hammerstein. It starred two excellent actors—Julie Andrews and Christopher Plummer.

Punctuating Titles

Show the title of a book, movie, play, television show, or website by using italics or underlining it.

Examples:
Sarah, Plain and Tall   or   Sarah, Plain and Tall
Peter and the Wolf   or   Peter and the Wolf
Sesame Street   or   Sesame Street

Put quotation marks around the title of a short work, such as a poem, song, short story, or book chapter.

Examples: "Dreams" is a poem by Langston Hughes.
We sang "Jingle Bells" and many other winter songs.
"The Monkey's Paw" is a scary short story by W.W. Jacobs.
In My Side of the Mountain, by Jean Craighead George, one of the chapters is called "The Old, Old Tree."

Proofreader's Symbols

Description	Symbol	Example
Make capital	≡	the car raced down the street.
Add something	∧	The car raced down street. the
Make lower case	/	The Car raced down the street.
Take something out	ꝺ	The car raced down the the street.
Check spelling	sp◯	The cor raced down the street.
Indent	¶	¶The car raced down the street.
Add end punctuation	⊙ ! ?	The car raced down the street⊙

Help Pages

Greek and Latin Roots and Their Meanings

Root	Meaning	Root	Meaning	Root	Meaning	Root	Meaning
able	able to	*co, com*	with	*im, in*	not	*pan*	all
amphi	both	*con*	with	*inter*	between	*phon*	sound
ante	before	*de*	take away	*less*	without	*photo*	light
anthropo	human	*di*	two	*mal*	bad	*port*	carry
anti	against	*dia*	across	*micro*	tiny	*post*	after
astro	star	*dict*	speak	*mis*	bad	*pre*	before
auto	self	*dis*	not	*mono*	one	*re*	again
bi	two	*ful*	full of	*morph*	form	*scrib*	write
biblio	book	*geo*	earth	*neo*	new	*script*	write
bio	life	*graph, gram*	written	*non*	not	*thermo*	heat
centri	center	*hemi*	half	*ology*	study of	*trans*	across
chrono	time	*hydro*	water	*ped*	foot	*tri*	three
circum	around	*ible*	able	*phobe*	fear	*un*	not

Figurative Language

A **simile** is a way to describe something by using a comparison. A simile compares two things using the words *like* or *as*.

Example: The baby is *as playful as a kitten*. (A baby is compared to a kitten.)

A **metaphor** compares two things but does not use *like* or *as*. It uses a form of the verb *be*.

Example: Joey is *a magnet for bad luck*. (He attracts bad luck.)

The **denotation** of a word is its most specific and exact meaning, the dictionary definition. The **connotation** of word is a symbolic or figurative meaning.

Example: Mrs. Beardsley has a big heart. (The word heart connotes kindness.)

The patient has an enlarged heart. (The word heart denotes an internal organ.)

Personification is a literary device in which an author gives human features to something non-human.

Example: A battalion of sunflowers stood at attention, facing the commanding officer. (On a farm, sunflowers grow in rows; they are rigid, like soldiers in formation, and the flower always turns toward the sun.)

An **idiom** is a saying with a figurative–not literal–meaning; the saying usually only has meaning within a specific culture.

Examples: We bought a used car, and it's a real lemon!
(refers to a car that has many problems or doesn't run)

At first I was angry, but I got over it.
(refers to letting go of something that was upsetting)

Help Pages

Spelling Rules
Adding Prefixes
When adding a prefix or joining two words, do not change the spelling of the base word.
Adding Suffixes that Begin with a Consonant

When adding a suffix that begins with a consonant, do not change the spelling of the base word.
Examples: joy + ful → joyful   wool + ly → woolly   agree + ment → agreement
     pain + ful → painful   sincere + ly → sincerely   govern + ment → government
Common Exceptions: argue + ment → argument   true + ly → truly   nine + th → ninth
     judge + ment → judgment   due + ly → duly   awe + ful → awful

Adding Suffixes that Begin with a Vowel
When a word ends in a **vowel + y**, add a suffix without changing the spelling of the base word. **Examples:** employ + er → employer   play + ing → playing   gray + est → grayest   enjoy + ment → enjoyment
When a word ends in **silent e**, usually drop the *e* to add a suffix that begins with a vowel. **Example:** love + able → lovable   (suffix begins with a vowel)
When a word ends in a **consonant + y** pattern, usually change the *y* to *i* when adding a suffix. **Example:** try + ed → tried   (ends in consonant + *y*; change the *y* to *i*) Do not change the *y* to *i* if the word ends in a vowel + *y* pattern or if the suffix is *ing*. **Examples:** destroy + ed → destroyed   (vowel + *y*)   hurry + ing → hurrying   (suffix is *ing*)

When a one-syllable word ends in the **cvc pattern (consonant - vowel - consonant)**, usually double the final consonant to add a suffix that begins with a vowel.
Examples: ship + ing → shipping   (suffix begins with a vowel)
     ship + ment → shipment   (suffix begins with a consonant)
     nut + y → nutty   (suffix is *y*)

When a one-syllable word ends in the **cvc pattern**, and the final consonant is *s*, *x* or *w*, do not double the final consonant.
Examples: mix + ing → mixing
     box + ed → boxed
     slow + er → slower

When a multi-syllable word ends in the **cvc pattern**, and the **accent is on the last syllable**, usually double the final consonant to add a suffix that begins with a vowel. **Example:** commit + ing → committing   (suffix begins with a vowel) **Common Exception:** prefer + able → preferable

Help Pages

Spelling Rules (continued)

Making Plurals

When a word **ends in s, x, z, ch, or sh** add -es to make the plural
   Examples: tax → taxes   wish → wishes

Many words that **end in f or fe,** change the f or fe to -ves.
   Examples: life → lives   thief → thieves
Other words that **end in f or ff** do not follow the rule for making plurals.
   Examples: cliff → cliffs   belief → beliefs

For words that **end in a consonant + o**, add an s to make the plural.
   Example: patio → patios
Other words that end in a consonant + o, add an es to make the plural.
   Example: tomato → tomatoes

Irregular plural nouns have a completely different spelling in the plural form.
   Examples: ox → oxen   goose → geese   louse → lice

Place i before e, except after c, or when sounded like /ā/ as in neighbor and weigh.
   Examples: mischief   receive   eight

There are many exceptions to spelling rules. If you are not sure of the spelling of a word, use a dictionary to check.

Analogies

An **analogy** is a way of comparing.
Example: mayor : city :: governor : state.   This is read: mayor is to city as governor is to state.

To solve an analogy, figure out the relationship between the two words.

   The *mayor* is the leader of the *city*. The *governor* is the leader of a *state*.

Example: lamb : sheep :: calf : _____   horse   piglet   cow   kitten

What is the relationship? A *lamb* is a baby *sheep*. The missing word must be *cow* because a *calf* is a baby cow.

In an **analogy**, the words may be compared in many ways.

Relationship	Example
synonyms	happy : joyful :: tall : high *Happy* and *joyful* are synonyms. *Tall* and *high* are synonyms too.
antonyms	thin : thick :: rich : poor *Thin* is the opposite of *thick*. *Rich* is the opposite of *poor*.
descriptions	bright : sunshine :: prickly : porcupine *Sunshine* is *bright*. A *porcupine* is *prickly*.
parts	wheels : bicycle :: legs : table A *bicycle* has *wheels*. A *table* has *legs*.
categories or subgroups	rabbit : mammal :: orange : fruit A *rabbit* is a type of *mammal*. An *orange* is a type of *fruit*.

Help Pages Index

A

Adjectives 69
Adverbs 68
  that tell how 68
  that tell to what extent 68
  that tell when 68
  that tell where 68
Analogies 75
Antecedent 64
Apostrophe 71

C

Commas 71
Complete predicate 70
Complete subject 70
Conjunctions 68
  coordinating 68
  correlative 68
  subordinating 68

D

Dashes 71
Declarative 70
Denotation 73
Direct object 64

E

Exclamatory 70

F

Figurative language 73
Fragments 69

G

Greek and Latin roots 73

I

Idiom 73
Imperative 70
Indirect object 64
Interjections 69
Interrogative 70
Irregular verbs 67

M

Metaphor 73

N

Nonrestrictive phrases 70
  punctuation 72
Nouns 64

O

Object of a preposition 64

P

Parts of speech 64
Perfect verb tense 67
Personal pronouns 65
Personification 73
Phrases, nonrestrictive 70
Phrases, restrictive 70
Possessive noun 64
Predicate 70
Predicate nominative 64
Predicate noun 64
Prepositions 69
Pronoun 64
  demonstrative 65, 66
  indefinite 65
  intensive 65, 66
  interrogative 65
  objective 65
  possessive 65
  reflexive 65, 66
  relative 65
  subjective 65
Proofreader's symbols 72
Punctuating nonrestrictive elements 72
Punctuating titles 72
Punctuation 71
  apostrophe 71
  comma 71
  dash 71
  semicolon 71

R

Restrictive phrases 70
Run-on sentences 69

S

Semicolon 71
Sentences 69
  features of a sentence 69
  fragments 69
  run-on sentences 69
Sentence structure 70
  complex 70
  compound 70
  simple 70
Sentence types 70
Simile 73
Simple predicate 70
Simple subject 70
Simple verb tense 67
Spelling rules 74
Subject 64, 70

T

Titles, punctuation 72

V

Verb 66
  action, intransitive 66
  action, transitive 66
  auxiliary 66
  being 66
  helping 66
  irregular 67
  linking 66
Verb tense 67

Common Core
ENGLISH GRAMMAR 6
& Mechanics

Answers to Lessons

	Lesson #1		Lesson #2		Lesson #3
1	A little red lighthouse… Fans of the book… Happily, it is still…	1	its / their / my, our, his, her, their, or your	1	…about the trip, a Greek island cruise, that he has already begun…
2	harsh	2	Since it is the birthplace of Abraham Lincoln…	2	cereal serial slay sleigh
3	us O them O They S	3	You're your	3	… plants…themselves. …cell…itself.
4	The fun things of summer. (crossed out)	4	but / and / yet (Any one.)	4	(Wyatt) scored…himself.
5	Answers may vary. These are the fun things of summer.	5	enthusiastic	5	The line…(wound)…
6	The batter usually takes a few warm up swings.	6	Nora wrote a poem for (me). She was only… published (it). They asked …(them). "I can… to (him).	6	subject (Answers will vary.) Rodney caught a catfish, a few carp, and a trout.
7	and	7	…soccer team (to) the… tournament	7	is starting
8	P C P Lena bakery Paris C C P macaron dessert Paul P C P basket Kia ground	8	C D B A	8	between pages
9	complement compliment	9	An old, slow tractor plowed up the dry, brittle stalks last Sunday.	9	Neither nor
10	Champ buries bones under his (doghouse).	10	…of France gave… …statue celebrates…	10	B A

	Lesson #4		Lesson #5		Lesson #6
1	will be preparing	1	…volleyball, swam in the ocean, and…	1	A) effect B) affect
2	antonyms	2	neither / nor	2	~~Lots of adventure and intrigue on a bicycle.~~
3	C B D A	3	An <u>enormous</u> <u>golden</u> dog poked its <u>cold</u>, <u>wet</u> nose…the <u>rotten</u> <u>wooden</u> fence.	3	(Answers will vary.) It involved lots of adventure and intrigue on a bicycle.
4	A <u>pack</u> …(roams)…	4	…<u>outside the boundaries</u>. boundaries	4	has prepared have prepared
5	it (runs) (elect) their	5	Jerome <u>bought</u> a baseball (mitt). Carina <u>baked</u> (tarts) for…	5	If / then
6	The <u>page winced</u>… <u>Rain pounded its fists</u>…	6	The cyclist <u>braked</u> (quickly.) (how)	6	Aiden and Levi are in the same gym class and play on the same rugby team.
7	or (and is also acceptable)	7	…<u>into our yard</u>. yard …<u>up the oak tree</u>. tree	7	…<u>brought</u> two sharpened pencils…
8	..(will sing) in the choir.	8	was rising	8	✓ A person who is…
9	…<u>neither</u> ate all of (its)…	9	alter — a table… altar — a verb… mussel — a noun… muscle — a shellfish…	9	is …and ~~was~~ out of gas… **or** had The car ~~has~~ two…
10	Oh no, I left… Hurry, I've got to…	10	studious enjoyable payment implied	10	The <u>dogs</u>..(have) eaten.

Lesson #7

1. weight — *i* before *e*
   conceive — except after *c*
   thief — or when...
2. lie
   lay
3. ...(behind) the elementary school
   school
4. ✓ im-
   ✓ dis-   ✓ non-
              ✓ in-
5. E
   F
   A
   B
   C
   D
6. will be dancing
7. (Cats)...themselves...
8. C   C   P
   kids baskets Snickers
   C   C   P
   Kit Kats rabbits Easter
9. Today, by the way, is...
   ..(on Saturday morning)..
10. quick at learning, bright

Lesson #8

1. (Answers may vary.)
   Grace called Alex so she could tell (Alex / Grace) the homework assignment.
2. simile
3. before
   unless
4. were lying
   was sleeping
5. amiable friendly affable
6. halves boxes tomatoes
7–8. a barnyard fowl
     someone who is afraid
9–10.
   G   F
   C   E
   B   D
   A

Lesson #9

1. Our dog, excited to go on a walk, wagged...
2. ...team (practices)...
   Mark Spitz and Michael Phelps (are)...
3. Example: It is against Roosevelt, one of our fiercest rivalries.
   (Sentences will vary.)
4. had challenged
   had challenged
5. isle — the passage...
   aisle — a small...
   allowed — a verb...
   aloud — an adverb...
6. C
7. not only
   but also
8. ..(libary) this $ummer... [sp]
   ..dog sitting...they think...
   ...from ms. Jeffers.
9. the apple (or *the lunchbox*)
   ...put it away...
10. ...swatted the hive...

	Lesson #10		Lesson #11		Lesson #12
1	…was served to (us).	1	C A D B	1	shabby decrepit rickety
2	its	2	Margaret's team entered the jump rope competition, but the event was rained out.	2	…landscape, rather than his self-portrait, with my savings.
3	as / as	3	admire thrifty	3	B A
4	controlled maintaining propeller occurrence feasted boxing	4	B A	4	A C B
5	A) solved B) dress C) are dressing D) have dressed E) carried F) have carried	5	..(into) our sails… sails	5	The movie that will be shown…
6	tomorrow	6	…benefits of exercise, *as everyone knows*, is being…	6	A) complete subject B) complete predicate (carried)
7	uncertainty	7	bias	7	subject coordinating
8	(They've all had swimming lessons.)	8	he we	8	~~Tried on my new swimsuit.~~ I tried on my new swimsuit.
9	There their	9	B A	9	has
10	(Answers may vary.) I can't wait for the sleepover at Chelsea's house.	10	insult a roller coaster bee sting	10	have

	Lesson #13		**Lesson #14**		**Lesson #15**
1	It's its	1	B C A D	1	<u>No one</u> his / her <u>Someone</u> him / her <u>Either</u> its / his / her
2	me O he P she P him O	2	Pig Pen magnet for dirt	2	is thinking had thought
3	study of time without	3	B A	3	You (understood) imperative
4	…<u>will have soccer practice at the high school field.</u>	4	is sails	4	Eli (or *Al*) …because ~~he~~ wanted…
5	Whose Who's	5	even though	5	is She ~~be~~… were We ~~was~~…
6	School (in case you haven't heard) is…	6	C A B	6	My (neighbor) along with his four dogs (visits)…
7	A) had scurried B) mapped C) was mapping D) drove E) was driving F) had driven	7	C	7	R (Chas) himself I (dog) itself R (Sabrina) herself
8	<u>Jamie always remembers his lunch money</u>, but he forgot it today.	8	flower : garden	8	C B A
9	<u>Jenna would not lend Jamie lunch money unless he promised to pay her back tomorrow.</u>	9	personification Example: The car spit out a puff of smoke. (Answers will vary.)	9	Example: Elijah wanted to go mountain biking although it looked like rain. (Sentences may vary.)
10	(unless)	10	You (understood)	10	anthrop(o)morphic human form

Lesson #16		Lesson #17		Lesson #18	
1	I (We)..ourselves. R (Jordan)..himself.	1	E C	1	the city (or *the bus*)
2	P P Friday Independence P C Ohio award P Environmental Protection Agency C ceremony	2	P ...none (have).. S ...most (has)...	2	am inviting will have invited
3	...throughout the lengthy program. throughout program	3	My mom will come and pick us up (whenever).. (Even though)...our car is already full.	3	..., as you can see,... ..., normally bold and dramatic,...
4	A *platter*...(awaits)...	4	B A	4	B D C F E A
5	around half tiny new	5	has ...she ~~have~~ our tickets.	5	them and us
6 – 7	A D B C	6	Example: Ella insisted the twins help clean up since they had made the mess in the first place. (Sentences may vary.)	6	~~All my cousins, aunts, uncles, and family friends.~~ Example: All my cousins, aunts, uncles, and family friends will be there. (Sentences may vary.)
		7	whom Who	7	marches
8	wipe out	8	Whoever whomever	8	A) wild B) energetic
9	B C A	9	She is my fairy godmother.	9	R We...ourselves... R They...themselves... I She...herself...
10	Example: Many their (Answers may vary.)	10	Aunt CeeCee fairy godmother	10	A

	Lesson #19		Lesson #20		Lesson #21
1	not only / but also both / and (Answers may vary.)	1	C . D ? A . B !	1	B A C
2	You (understood) Jonathan	2	your yours her hers their ours	2	…hanukkah gift⊙ sp Unfortuneately…Summer. …I we could…to soccer. play
3	…, not the movies, … …freestyle, not the…	3	navy it (does) flock it (escorts)	3	them We his
4	…winking flirtatiously… personification	4	…, not walk it, …	4	Everyone…his… Many are
5	Who he	5	My (cousin) who lives…	5	harmful
6	create has created will have created	6	affect — a noun… effect — a verb… dissent — to disagree… descent — the act…	6	reflexive—She dressed… intensive—He carried…
7	is	7	will be appearing will have appeared	7	B F A D G C E
8	exclamatory	8	lobbyist employment happiness replied babyish playable	8	E C
9	(She)…herself. (They)…themselves.	9	…(outside of Chicago)…	9	Anne's (or Sis's)
10	oven	10	she	10	both ~~Really delicious…syrup.~~

	Lesson #22		Lesson #23		Lesson #24
1	I (We)…ourselves R (He)…himself…	1	…beckoning everyone to dinner with its long wispy fingers. personification	1	challenging difficult distinctive peculiar grimace sneer admire envy
2	(Answers will vary.) the teachers …like ~~they~~ told us.	2	they	2	C
3	B G C D H A E F	3	hoarse — a four-legged… horse ✗ describes… forth — an adverb… fourth — a noun…	3	Example: Chromosomes carry the genetic material and they are located in the nucleus of a cell. (Answers may vary.)
4	B	4	B A	4	E C
5	D	5	whoever Whoever	5	me she
6	Example: I crossed to the other side of the street because I was afraid of that barking dog. (Sentence may vary.)	6		had laid	have laid	will have laid
had forgiven	have forgiven	will have forgiven
had bitten	have bitten	will have bitten		6	The (babies) themselves… The (coach) himself…
7	who whom	7	is	7	…, never pecans, … …, not a present, …
8	…, not a pizza, … …, not just by text messages,…	8	(on) the ice (for) a minute (between) each performance (in) each event (except) ice dancing	8	chimney
9	P P Tom Hanks Sheriff Woody P C P *Toy Story* film Pixar Animation Studio P California	9	(colony) (exits) It (mosquitoes) (sense) They	9	has won have won
10	complex simple	10	A) pushy B) assertive	10	whether / or

	Lesson #25		Lesson #26		Lesson #27
1	(governor) his (herd) it is (Butterflies) emerge	1	A F E D C B	1	saved buys ~~saves~~ or ~~bought~~ hopes began ~~hoped~~ or ~~begins~~
2	the ball …so I picked ~~it~~ up.	2	B C A	2	will be feeding will be going
3	had eaten / have eaten / will have eaten had dealt / have dealt / will have dealt had swum / have swum / will have swum	3	…winter only <u>tightened its stranglehold</u>… winter	3	has trained had trained will have trained
4	The <u>jeans</u>…(are)… Ava's red <u>hat</u>…(is)…	4	prevent	4	What whom Whose
5	Nicolas (or Alfonso) …and now ~~he~~ is…	5	You (understood)	5	He
6	~~Received the second most number of votes.~~ Example: Thomas Jefferson had received the second highest number of votes. (Sentences may vary.)	6	<u>auto</u>(biography) the self-written story of a person's life	6	pour ╳ (verb)… pore ╳ (verb)… hole ╳ (adjective)… whole ╳ (noun)…
7	✓ You are a couch…	7	A B	7	I (cheerleaders) themselves R (She) herself I (We) ourselves
8	will have taught	8	is are	8	…, not the gas-guzzler, … …, not weed the garden, …
9	She S Who S	9	I R	9	critique
10	B C A	10	my bike (or my helmet) …but ~~it~~ is fine.	10	✓ Tech Creation Learning Tools for Kids

	Lesson #28		Lesson #29		Lesson #30
1	..., since you rode to school with her, ... No, she didn't...	1	anachronism opposition... antiwar ⟍ ⟋ an animal... amphibian ⟋ ⟍ something...	1	D A C B
2	were They ~~are~~... **or** want ...they ~~wanted~~...	2	wherever Since (Answers may vary.)	2	...masks, we saw... ...below, if we held...
3	~~Successfully drove out the Spaniards.~~ Answers may vary. The Aztecs successfully drove out the Spaniards.	3 — 4	E D C G F B H A	3 — 4	B G F C D E _ A
4	are was				
5	its their	5	were finishing had finished	5	B
6	Mr. Weber, who... The team that...	6	Which What whom	6	us We
7	is am are be being was were been	7	Emily's (or Meredith's) ...but she's moving...	7	✓ The rusty old... ✓ A full harvest...
8	B D A C	8	Example: The Maya were able to develop the concept of zero because they were capable mathematicians. (Answers may vary.)	8	their
9	✓ A synonym... ✓ *Ominous* means...	9	R You yourselves I Megan herself R They themselves	9	A) tricked B) cheated
10	adjective	10	Many Everyone (Answers may vary.)	10	R themselves They R himself boy I ourselves we